JB JOSSEY-BASS™
A Wiley Brand

Best-Ever Directory of Special Events

FIFTH EDITION

Scott C. Stevenson, Editor

WILEY

Best Ever Directory of Special Events
— 5th Edition

Published by

Stevenson, Inc.

P.O. Box 4528 • Sioux City, Iowa • 51104
Phone 712.239.3010 • Fax 712.239.2166
www.stevensoninc.com

Best Ever Directory of Special Events — 5th Edition

TABLE OF CONTENTS

Best Ever Directory of Special Events, Fifth Edition.
Edited by Scott C. Stevenson.
© 2010 Stevenson, Inc. Published 2010 by Stevenson, Inc.

To make your event even more memorable for attendees, engage them. As this chapter illustrates, there are a multitude of ways you can get attendees to be active participants in your events — playing games, participating in contests and more.

Scrabble® Challenge Tests Skill, Raises Big Bucks

Frontier College (Toronto, Ontario, Canada) hosts an annual Scrabble® Corporate Challenge to raise funds to improve literacy rates across Canada. The event raises attention for the college and the cause, as well as major funds, bringing in nearly $1 million over five years.

"With more than 40 percent of Canadians struggling to read and write, our Scrabble® Corporate Challenge is the perfect antidote," says Sherry Campbell, college president. "Having Bay Street executives roll up their sleeves to play Scrabble®, shows corporate Canada's desire to be a part of the literacy solution."

The 2009 corporate challenge, presented by TMX Group, consisted of 40 teams of four players playing a rousing match of the popular word-crafting game.

The competition "creates a networking opportunity for like-minded wordsmiths from companies representing banking, legal, accounting, data services, technology and wealth management sectors to gather in support of Frontier College's literacy programs," says Meredith Roberts, Frontier's manager of special events and media relations.

Teams of four players paid $5,000 to compete. Local corporations funded employee teams, and some companies donated entry fees for other groups to participate, such as a team from the public library.

At the 2009 event, six regionally and nationally recognized Scrabble® champions were on hand to act as ringers for teams to enlist assistance — considered a power play — when choosing a word from their existing tiles for an additional donation.

Teams competed for title of best individual player, winner of their conference (e.g., legal conference, accounting conference) and highest-scoring team. The team deemed the final winner overall took home the Scrabble® TMX Cup and bragging rights.

In addition to the corporate challenge, event organizers encourage a grassroots Scrabble® effort for individuals to participate in known as the Scrabble® Friends & Family Challenge. In this effort, individuals can coordinate a neighborhood Scrabble® challenge raising funds for local literacy programs.

Source: Meredith Roberts, Manager-Special Events & Media Relations, Frontier College Foundation, Toronto, Ontario, Canada. Phone (416) 923-3591. E-mail: mroberts@frontiercollege.ca

Black Tie Monopoly Passes Go, Collects $175,000

How far does the board game theme go in the American Red Cross of the Delmarva Peninsula's (Wilmington, DE) Black Tie Monopoly and Monte Carlo Night?

"The hotel does ice sculptures in the shape of Monopoly pieces — the hat, the horse, the thimble," says Glenn Barnhill, chief development officer. "The food is themed, too. The Oriental Avenue features all Asian dishes. The Boardwalk has fries, pizza and saltwater taffy."

The motif of the uber-popular Hasbro board game goes beyond mere artwork and decorations. Opportunities for corporate sponsorship, the event's primary source of revenue, are sold as properties on the game board.

Because organizers purchase rights to the Monopoly trademark, specially made game sets featuring sponsor names and logos can be produced for guests to use over the course of the evening. Barnhill says that in any given year, up to 20 tables will compete in a two-round tournament, culminating with the crowning of an annual Monopoly champion.

Just as important, though, are the blackjack and roulette tables of Monte Carlo Night. Often the evening's most popular activities, the games use chips redeemable for tickets in raffles with prizes like flat screen TV's, elegant dinners, and use of beach houses/condos.

And in true mogul style, the night is rounded out with (and revenues significantly augmented by) silent and live auctions featuring items drawn from the community chest.

The event is not so different from other black tie fundraisers, but the tie-in to Park Place and Boardwalk makes a difference, says Barnhill.

"Adding a theme makes gala events more intriguing and inviting to guests," he says, and on that 'the facts back him up. Black Tie Monopoly has attracted considerable attention over its five-year run, and though the 2009 event suffered from challenging economic conditions, the Red Cross has consistently netted $100,000 to $175,000.

At a Glance —	
Event Type:	Themed Gala
Gross:	$155,000 to $230,000
Costs:	$55,000
Net Income:	$100,000 to $175,000
Volunteers:	80
Planning:	8 months
Attendees:	325
Revenue Sources:	Corporate sponsorships, silent auctions, ticket sales, sales of gaming chips

Source: Glenn Barnhill, Chief Development Officer, American Red Cross of the Delmarva Peninsula, Wilmington, DE. Phone (302) 472-6251. E-mail: Gbarnhill@redcrossdelmarva.org

Hospital's Idol Contest Boosts Morale, Taps Talents

At University Hospital Case Medical Center (UHCMC) in Cleveland, OH, a contest that plays on the popularity of the American Idol phenomenon has revved up morale and bonded volunteers, patients and staff like none other.

Barb Nalette, director of volunteer services, answers a few questions about this exciting event:

Who participates in the UHCMC Idol Contest and how many people try out?

"The UHCMC Idol Contest is geared to hospital staff, volunteers and physicians throughout our health system. In all about 100 individuals auditioned for the opportunity to become the first UHCMC Idol in 2006 and about 80 individuals to become the second UHCMC Idol in 2008. The contestants came from a wide variety of both patient and non-patient care areas of the hospital."

What was the purpose of this event? What did it do for your organization?

"UHCMC is a very large health system. The president of the hospital asked the hospital's auxiliary to consider what its members could do to assist with employee engagement. When the auxiliary first presented the proposal to the senior leadership of the hospital they were unsure of the possibility of its success.

"The overwhelming participation and enjoyment of the event has made it one of the most successful hospital events."

Who was invited to the event where contestants competed?

"The entire hospital community and guests of the contestants were invited to attend the two shows held at midday to attract the most people. The auxiliary produced two shows — the semi-finals and the finals. A stage was constructed in the hospital's atrium where the contestants, ages 20 to 60, performed.

"The hospital's president was the emcee for the semi-finals and the 25 semifinalists enjoyed being introduced by him. The audience consisted of friends, family, co-workers of the contestants and the general hospital public. They made signs to support their contestant and came out in great force!

"The finals consisted of the five finalists (selected after the semifinals by a combination of judges' and audience votes). The finalists dressed for the show (instead of wearing the scrubs they wore during the semifinals), sang with piano accompaniment and the show was emceed by a professional in the Cleveland community.

"After the performances of the contestants, the emcee encouraged people from the audience to sing while the voting and ballot counting took place. The finalists were judged solely by the audience."

Were you surprised by the talent exhibited?

"Who knew we had so many talented people working and volunteering here? We were overwhelmed by the quality of the talent and are certain we have uncovered and fostered people's creative abilities."

Were there prizes involved? If so, please explain.

"The UHCMC Idol Contest winner received a cash prize of $1,000 and a recording session at a local studio. The first runner-up received $300 and the three remaining finalists received $100 American Express Gift Cards. The 25 semifinalists were given a gift for participating. The auxiliary provided the prizes.

"When the finalists were announced, the president presented the women with flowers and the men with a gift."

What advice would you offer another organization that might attempt an event such as this?

"Planning and advertising are key to the success of a program of this scope. We started planning months before the event and advertised using teasers — changing the signs posting the event almost weekly."

Source: Barbara Nalette, Director of Volunteer Services, University Hospital Case Medical Center, Cleveland, OH. Phone (216) 844-1504. E-mail: Barbara.Nalette@uhhospitals.org

Teams Pull Together to Raise Funds

Talk about teamwork! Teams of supporters literally pulled together recently to raise funds for the Community Mediation Center (Harrisonburg, VA).

The organization hosted its second annual plane pull with 14 teams literally pulling a plane — a King Air turbo prop weighing in at 8,000 pounds — 150 feet.

"We wanted something fun that people were interested in being a part of," says Amy Good, assistant director. "It is a lot of fun to pull a plane, and people always want to come back the next year."

Registered teams are given a pull time and asked to arrive 30 minutes early to sign release forms and receive instructions. After the team pulls the plane, the pull time is recorded and publicly posted.

Teams of five to eight people compete in one of three categories: fastest pull time, most dynamic team (costumes were encouraged) or lightest weight (the participants were weighed).

Other activities at the plane pull included face painting and free plane rides for children, live music and food vendors.

Cost to register was $500 for teams sponsored by an organization or $25 per person for those competing as a group of friends. The event grossed $7,300.

Source: Amy Good, Assistant Director, Community Mediation Center, Harrisonburg, VA. Phone (540) 434-0059. E-mail: amy@weworkitout.org

Trivia Event Dubbed 'Friendraiser'

Trivia night parties are near and dear to the hearts of St. Louis, MO, residents. The events are so popular, in fact, that St. Louisans have developed at least one website (www.trivianights.net) dedicated to promoting trivia events.

When event organizers with the St. Louis Arc (St. Louis, MO) decided to join in the buzz and host a trivia night, they looked beyond its fundraising potential to tap it as a "friendraising" event.

While the event is not the highest earning fundraiser for the Arc, it is by far the most popular, says Lindsey Harris, special events manager.

Nearly 400 people attended the 2009 event, the seventh annual trivia event for the St. Louis Arc. The event has become so popular that organizers sell only entire tables versus single seats. Eight-person tables sell for $200 each.

"Our trivia event provides an inexpensive way to support the St. Louis Arc while inviting friends and family to find out more about what we do," Harris says. "Many trivia night attendees become supporters in other ways throughout the year by volunteering, donating auction items and raising awareness about the organization."

To offer a trivia event that is well attended, plus a great way to raise friends:

- Form a program committee that will help develop the categories and questions for the trivia event. Having a diverse group of people will ensure that the questions will please and challenge a wide audience.
- Coordinate volunteers who can be engaging and humorous emcees throughout the evening.
- Create a schedule noting the timing of the evening to include the length of each trivia round, activities between rounds, food and drink service and stick to it!
- Develop a theme for the night and incorporate it into the invite, decorations, volunteer attire and trivia questions.

Source: Audrey Ting, Coordinator of Volunteers and Community Outreach; Lindsey Harris, Special Events Manager, St. Louis Arc, St. Louis, MO. Phone (314) 569-2211. E-mail: ATing@slarc.org

At a Glance —	
Event Type:	Trivia Night
Gross:	$16,900
Costs:	$4,900
Net Income:	$12,000
Volunteers:	45
Planning:	5 to 6 months
Attendees:	400
Revenue Sources:	Entry fee of $200 per table, silent auction, 50/50 raffle
Unique Feature:	Attendees learn about other ways to support the nonprofit during the evening

Content not available in this edition

Trivia Nights Growing in Popularity

Twelve years ago, the Bishop Kelley High School (BKHS) of Tulsa, OK, held its first trivia night in a cafeteria with 20 tables. Today, the event fills two gymnasiums and sells out 1,180 spots at 118 tables within a few short weeks.

"A lot goes into Trivia Night, but it never seems like anyone is working that hard. People are talking and laughing and the money just comes in," says Christy Grisaffe, one of the event's main organizers. She says the school raises as much as $25,000 every year through table sales ($150 regular, $600 corporate), food and beverage sales, and other raffles and contests.

Much of the event's success stems from the loyal following it has built over time. Grisaffe says 70 percent of tables go to repeat participants.

Another key is the fundraiser's two-events-in-one structure. Participants choose either the "serious" room where title contention is in the air and a quiet, serious atmosphere reigns, or the "crazy" room where socialization and celebration are the main objective.

Grisaffe says the event benefits from a long-standing tradition of support from each year's 25th anniversary class. Class members write the questions, serve as emcees, organize concessions, collaborate with the planning committee, and typically provide about half of the 100 volunteers required.

"It's like organizing a big party that everyone is waiting for," Grisaffe says of the planning process. "Once you get a trivia night started, it just keeps going."

Source: Christy Grisaffe, Trivia Night Organizer, Tulsa, OK. Phone: (918) 809-5702. E-mail: Trivia@bkelleyhs.org

Poker Event Serves Up a Full House

The Showdown for St. Louis Arc Texas Hold 'Em Tournament is a fundraising smash. In its fifth year, the annual event at St. Louis Arc (St. Louis, MO) draws 130 guests and raises $25,000 to support the nonprofit's programs that support those with developmental disabilities with pertinent services, family support and advocacy.

The organization trains 35 dealers to entertain guests at 17 tables for the one-night affair. Organizers offer tips on how to plan a successful poker event:

- **Find expert dealer trainers.** Contact a local casino or organization that will train your dealers as a volunteer effort toward your event.

- **Pre-train dealers.** One week prior to the annual poker event, event organizers at St. Louis Arc bring together experienced dealers from previous events and trainees for a night of learning. Dealers learn the basics of dealing a poker game, plus style and finesse for card handling. This training is mandatory for all dealers at the St. Louis Arc event and ensures that dealers are ready to fulfill their task at the tables.

- **Pair new dealers with experienced dealers.** Pairing dealers is an excellent way to introduce new dealers to your event. Having an experienced dealer sidekick allows new dealers a level of comfort and an opportunity to share the role while learning. Pairing also ensures that rules are followed.

- **Tap local businesses and young professional groups when recruiting new dealers for the event.** St. Louis Arc considers local businesses and young professional groups when seeking the right personalities for dealers of the evening. Look to seasoned volunteers to become pit bosses for the event. Pit bosses must be fluent regarding the rules of poker and intervene when rules are questioned.

Source: Audrey Ting, Coordinator of Volunteers and Community Outreach, and Lindsey Harris, Special Events Manager, St. Louis Arc, St. Louis, MO. Phone (314) 569-2211. E-mail: ATing@slarc.org or LHarris@slarc.org

The reply card, left, and flyer for the Texas Hold 'Em Poker Tournament for the St. Louis Arc (St. Louis, MO), emphasize the event's theme.

Content not available in this edition

Content not available in this edition

A Winning Bet: Casino Parties

An odds-on favorite party is one with casino games that boost fundraising or just add to the fun. For yours to be a success, don't gamble on the outcome — heed these tips from Crystal Clarke, customer services manager, All Star Productions (Arlington, TX):

✓ **Offer prizes.** "A successful casino party always has something for people to look forward to at the end, whether a raffle, drawing or an auction," Clarke says. "When the guests don't have an incentive to actually play the games, they're not as excited."

✓ **Include the favorites.** Be sure to have blackjack tables, "a very simple game that 90 percent of the people understand," Clarke says. Roulette is also easy to learn, and craps, while more complicated, is typically the highest-energy game and can really get the crowd going. Texas Hold 'em is popular, although since players are betting against each other and not the house, it's tough to amass many chips for prizes.

✓ **Don't assume everyone will want to play.** Plan enough gambling spots for 70 percent of attendees. Offer other entertainment, such as a video arcade arena, dancing and a DJ for other attendees.

✓ **Institute a maximum bet.** "This keeps things fair on all the tables, especially when you're giving prizes," Clarke says.

✓ **If hiring an outside company, get questions answered beforehand.** A company's quote should include setup/tear-down, dealers, a pit boss and all tools necessary to play the games. The pit boss should walk around and be a liaison with both you and the dealers. You should offer water and sodas to the staff working the party, but you should never be expected to provide food. Most casino parties last about three hours and seem to fizzle out after that.

Source: Crystal Clarke, Customer Services Manager, All Star Productions, Arlington, TX. Phone (214) 642-6468. E-mail: crystal@allstarproductions.net

Blue Jeans Raise Some Green as Internal Fundraiser

If a major fundraising component of your budget falls through, put together your organization's most creative people to come up with a replacement that generates needed funds and welcome awareness.

At Make-A-Wish Foundation of Illinois (Chicago, IL), Jessica Miller, communications manager, says the development staff members were looking to fill the gap left by the unexpected loss of a significant corporate event and only had a few months to do so. They came up with a coordinated campaign called Jeans for Wishes.

"On a smaller scale we had always suggested this as one of the ways schools could raise funds for us," Miller says. "The year 2009 was our first effort to rally schools and companies in a campaign we ran internally."

For the first Jeans for Wishes effort, 60 teams raised a combined $88,000.

Here's how the fundraiser works:

Teams (companies and schools) sign up at www.jeansforwishes.org, pledging to collect a certain dollar amount from people interested in being allowed to wear blue jeans on a designated day or for a designated period. Once a team commits, the team representative receives a starter kit that includes marketing materials and stickers for each employee or student who donates. The money raised is donated to the foundation.

Miller says one reason the campaign is such a success is because of its flexibility. Teams decide the donation amount and the designated time or day based on the needs of their own group (e.g., $1/day, $5/day or $20/week).

Another reason for success? The personal connection provided to participants. Miller says participants are able to send messages of encouragement directly to children whose wishes will be granted through the campaign via the website. "There is an immediate con-nection to the Make-A-Wish mission as soon as people hear they can send messages of encouragement. Being able to connect directly with those who will benefit from their donations has been a great motivator."

The goal for the 2010 Jeans for Wishes Campaign is $100,000.

Source: Jessica Miller, Make-A-Wish Foundation of Illinois, Chicago, IL. Phone (312) 602-9412. E-mail: Miller@wishes.org.

Five Tips for Success in a Pay-for-privilege Campaign

The Make-A-Wish Foundation of Illinois's (Chicago, IL) Jeans for Wishes campaign is a straightforward way to raise funds, though that doesn't mean there is no effort required. Jessica Miller, communications manager, says the following tips can help boost the success of similar campaigns:

1. **Utilize your network.** This is a great opportunity for those people who might not be in a position to donate a large sum of their own to have a large impact. Volunteers, clients, current students or recent graduates are all in a position to engage their employers, community groups and schools to participate.

2. **Plan ahead.** Many schools need information on fundraisers at the beginning of the school year. Similarly, some companies do a jeans program regularly for a variety of charities. Either way, your organization is just one of many being considered for inclusion. It's important to give prospective participants information far enough in advance to be considered in the decision-making process.

3. **Promote matching.** Miller says many of 2009's participant companies had matching options that doubled or tripled their employees' contributions.

4. **Make a connection.** Jeans for Wishes participants are able to reach out to beneficiaries of their donations via e-mail through the campaign website.

5. **Add variety to your marketing.** This campaign uses calling and mailing a postcard to groups who participated last year, a public relations campaign to reach schools and businesses in their service area, social networking components and e-mail communications to the organization's constituents.

Best Ever Directory of Special Events — 5th Edition

EVENTS GEARED TO WOMEN

There are times when it may be in your organization's best interests to reach out to a single gender. Once that decision has been made — for any number of reasons — there are dozens of gender-specific events from which you can select. The following events are geared to females.

Ladies-only Event Offers Fun for Women of All Ages

Women took center stage — and every seat in the place — as the Ronald McDonald House of Chapel Hill (Chapel Hill, NC) hosted its fourth annual Girls Just Wanna Have Fun fundraiser.

In a night filled with indulgences, women chose from massages, manicures, facials, tarot card readings, body painting and energy healings.

The $65 admission included hors d'oeuvres, a chocolate fondue fountain and two beverages.

Guests also got their shopping fix as they checked out the latest fashions and participated in a handbag auction, silent auction and a raffle for a seven-night, all-inclusive trip to Mexico.

"This is a unique event for the (Chapel Hill, Raleigh and Durham, NC) area in that it is geared exclusively to women of all ages," says Elizabeth Hullender, special events manager. "This is a great event for mothers and daughters to attend together, co-workers to attend, and it really gives all of those hardworking women a night tailored just for them."

Sponsorships and ticket sales/donations were the primary income sources, raising $14,200 and $11,735, respectively. The silent auction raised $4,055, and raffle, $2,440.

To publicize the event, staff posted information on the organization's website; did radio interviews; made public service announcements and a television appearance; and sent invitations to donors and past attendees.

Source: Elizabeth Hullender, Special Events Manager, Ronald McDonald House of Chapel Hill, Chapel Hill, NC. Phone (919) 913-2040. E-mail: elizabeth.hullender@ chapelhillrmh.net

At a Glance —	
Event Type:	Ladies' Night Out
Gross:	$35,460
Costs:	$13,500
Net Income:	$21,960
Volunteers:	72
Planning:	3 months
Attendees:	300
Revenue Sources:	Ticket sales, sponsorships, silent auction, raffle, donations
Unique Feature:	Caters to female audience with facials, handbag auctions and chocolate fondue

Fundraising Is in the Bag for Popular Purse Parties

When a woman sees another woman with a great purse, what's the first thing she asks? "Where did you get that!" That's just one reason to host a fundraising event in which great purses and handbags take center stage.

Realizing the current trend of colorful handbags and purses had women talking, officials with Kinship Partners (Brainerd, MN) created a unique event that features one-of-a-kind, celebrity and designer handbags.

In its third season, Purses for Partners raised $10,000 in April 2010 to benefit the Kinship Partners, an organization dedicated to youth mentoring.

This year, the Purses for Partners luncheon featured a luncheon including both silent and live auctions where 156 tickets at $25 each were sold and 155 purses were auctioned. Additionally, two specialty handbags were raffled at the event.

Elise Mink, marketing coordinator, tells more about securing handbags and managing this event:

✓ Event planners work with area businesses throughout the year to secure handbag donations for the event as well as gift certificates and gift items that are included within the handbags.

✓ To secure designer bags, event planners contact design houses throughout the country who give generously to the event. Mary Frances Accessories is a handbag design firm that creates hand-embellished bags and has given generously to Kinship Partners for their handbag event.

✓ Celebrity bags often are solicited from area celebrities. This year's celebrity donations came from local celebrities Jessica Miles and Liz Collin.

✓ Themed bags were also available for auction. For example, this year one purse was given a beach theme that included a beach towel, flip flops and a bottle of wine. Another bag was geared to girls and included a girl's purse filled with nail polish, lip gloss and a journal.

✓ Surprise! When a handbag is auctioned off, the purse is delivered to the winning guest and inside they find a surprise gift from a local vendor including items such as jewelry, gift certificates, lotions and more.

For organizations considering introducing trendy handbags to their next fundraiser, Mink advises holding the event near Mother's Day to ensure high attendance of local grandmothers, mothers and daughters. Start early, she says, to secure not only the purses and handbags, but support from area businesses to fill the bags with donated gift certificates, jewelry, perfumes, chocolates and additional perks.

Source: Elise Mink, Marketing Coordinator, Kinship Partners, Brainerd, MN. Phone (218) 829-4606. E-mail: marketing@kinshippartners.org.

Member Boot Camp Brings Together Women Entrepreneurs

Staff with the Greater Phoenix Chamber of Commerce (Phoenix, AZ) team up with Susan Ratliff Presents LLC to offer members and local female entrepreneurs a boot camp of education and motivation.

The Women Entrepreneurs Small Business Boot Camp is designed to offer a powerful day of world-class insights, cutting-edge success strategies, practical tools and relevant topics for women in business.

The event, which draws some 200 attendees, includes two keynote speakers and nine seminars guiding female entrepreneurs with advice on marketing to ethnic audiences, turning customer service into cash, viral marketing, shattering stress and more.

Ratliff answers questions about the event and offers tips for catering to a female audience:

What unique challenges do women entrepreneurs face that are addressed at this event?

"This conference has a succinct theme: no theory, philosophy or fluff, just an arsenal of ideas and practical ammunition to help battle women's most difficult business challenges. This educational conference tackles the issues that affect profits and productivity. With that said, our focus is to provide practical, relevant tips, tools and strategies these business owners can immediately implement the very next day. We address the basic profit-generating topics like sales, marketing, publicity, advertising, business planning and finances. Attendees leave with an immense amount of value for the $89 entry fee."

What are your top tips for catering to a female crowd at an event such as this?

"Our format is unique in several ways. We only showcase women speakers, most of whom are local, successful business owners. This way the attendees can actually visit them at their place of business after the event. We offer an expo element to the conference including 45 to 50 exhibits that showcase business resources to the attendees.

Additionally, we offer a retail row of products and services that women love such as clothing, jewelry, make-up and more. I invented a networking kiosk that stands in the foyer of the exhibit area and has room for 300 business cards. Attendees put a stack of cards in a slot

and take whatever other cards interest them — offering a great networking opportunity. We host an after-party called the Meet the Speakers Reception where the women can get up close and personal to the speakers at a cocktail party. Instead of a simple program, we provide a program binder that has all the speakers handouts inside, along with speaker biographies, sponsor ads etc. The binder allows the participants a way to get everyone's information even if they cannot attend each session."

Sources: Debbie Drotar, Greater Phoenix Chamber of Commerce, 201 Phoenix, AZ. Phone (602) 495-2195.
E-mail: ddrotar@phoenixchamber.com.
Website: www.phoenixchamber.com Susan Ratliff, Susan Ratliff Presents LLC, Phoenix, AZ. Phone (602) 437-3634.
E-mail: Susan@susanratliff.com. Website: www.susanratliff.com

Content not available in this edition

Girls Nite Out: Drawing Women to Your Event

Since its inception in 2007, the Girls Nite Out event (Northfield, MN) has drawn nearly 500 women for an evening of shopping, sales and female bonding, all for a good cause. More than 50 local businesses stay open late on a Saturday to offer special discounts on merchandise and services as part of the downtown shopping and social event.

The evening of the event, attendees gather at Northfield's Bridge Square to buy $10 wristbands that gain them admission to the specialty shops lining Division Street, plus special perks of the night including facials, makeovers, Tarot readings, appetizers, in-store drawings and manicures as well as special discounts from 5 to 9 p.m.

"When we started this event, we just wanted to have a great night for women where they could let loose and have a night off," says Ally Beyer, event co-chair. "It has become a yearly highly anticipated tradition for many groups of friends. It is the most amazing feeling to be at The Grand and to look around at the ages ranging from 21 to 80, everyone having a blast. It truly is a remarkable event and a wonderful way to say thank-you to the women of Northfield."

Not only do local businesses benefit from the event, a local charitable cause receives a portion of the proceeds from ticket sales each year. The recipient for the most recent event is the nonprofit Women in Northfield Giving Support (WINGS).

The event-planning committee works for months orchestrating the event, says Beyer, who shares innovative tips for drawing more women to your next event:

- **Advertise with flair.** Advertise in surrounding area newspapers with eye-catching colors and details about the event. The Girls Nite Out committee worked with a local artist to design a female-friendly invitation that became the impetus for the group's posters and advertisements.
- **Give attendees something new each year.** Add one new exciting thing to draw people in from the previous year, such as a $1,000 shopping spree grand prize.
- **Posters, Posters, Posters.** Put up posters in local businesses at least six weeks before your event to get people excited!
- **Build support, excitement from the inside out.** Be sure to have a solid committee with go-getters. Delegate tasks and work together as a team. That, Beyer says, is what made Girls Nite Out Northfield such a huge success.

Source: Ally Beyer, Co-Chair, Girls Nite Out, Northfield, MN.

Mother-daughter Luncheon Benefits Nonprofits and Businesses

Bringing mothers and daughters together turned out to be just the boost the Junior League of Galveston County (Galveston, TX) — and area businesses — needed.

Known for established annual events like a holiday ball, Junior League members wanted a new way to raise money and get their name out in the community, says Jill Kaale, 2008-'09 ways and means chairman. With only five months to plan, they decided to hold their first-ever Tickled Pink Mother-Daughter Tea & Style Show May 9, 2009.

Featuring a fashion show, light lunch and a boutique selling fun and funky women's clothing and gifts, the day raised $10,000 and drew 350 attendees, about one-third were members, Kaale says.

"The appeal was that this event honored real women of all ages, shapes and sizes. It's just a celebration of womanhood," Kaale says.

A bonus: A professional photographer was on hand to take family photos. Low-cost photo packages were available, and all ticket packages included free portraits.

Selling tickets to the event was a bit of a challenge, not because of lack of popularity, but because the Junior League's offices had been flooded when Hurricane Ike devastated Galveston in September 2008. Even though Kaale had to handle all ticket sales through her personal phone and e-mail address, reservations kept coming in, she says. Single tickets were $50, and special ticket packages ranged from $125 to $1,000.

To cut down on workload and promote reestablishment of Galveston businesses, planners held the event at the historic Hotel Galvez on Galveston Island. "It really cut down on the work we had to do, and they gave us a great rate," she says. "Everything was catered, they took care of set-up and tear down.... And the atmosphere was just beautiful."

The event's boutique was another unique community partnership, featuring nine local merchants. "They were all really pleased with the business they did there. Although we didn't ask that they donate a portion of their proceeds to the Junior League this year, we usually do. We probably will next year, when the event gets bigger," says Kaale.

Contact: Jill Kaale, Junior League of Galveston County, Galveston, TX. Phone (281) 309-1968. E-mail: JillLKaale@aol.com

At a Glance —	
Event Type:	Luncheon and style show
Gross:	$16,000
Costs:	$6,000
Net Income:	$10,000
Volunteers:	15
Planning:	5 months
Attendees:	350
Revenue Sources:	Ticket sales, sponsorships, program ads
Unique Feature:	Community businesses engaged through boutique, fashion show

Bingo! Togs & Tots Bingo Luncheon Draws Crowds

The Dallas Children's Advocacy Center League hosts a rousing day of bingo each year to raise awareness and funds for the Dallas Children's Advocacy Center (DCAC) of Dallas, TX.

The Togs & Tots Bingo Luncheon is an all-women event where up to 400 attendees — each of whom paid $100 a ticket or is a guest of a table sponsor — play eight to 10 games of bingo.

While bingo is a draw in itself, what really brings in the crowd is the enormous amount of prizes — nearly 500 donated gifts ranging from $25 to $1,000 in value — says Mary Blake Meadows, DCAC League member and former event chair: "It makes quite a statement when guests arrive and see an entire wall of colorful gift bags."

Guests are encouraged to wear Halloween costumes and vie for prizes at the October event. "One year a group came dressed as cheerleaders with a DCAC monogram on their sweaters and wrote and performed a cheer," says Meadows.

Here she shares tips for holding a successful bingo:

✓ Offer a pre-set salad lunch so tables can be set with the meal before guests arrive.

✓ Offer at least eight to 10 games of bingo to allow guests to interact and feel they've gotten their money's worth.

✓ Play bingo games that require a longer period of time to gain a bingo such as blackout.

✓ Build in excitement boosters such as giving prizes to the two people seated to the left and two on the right of anyone calling a bingo.

✓ Allow guests to buy additional bingo cards for $10 each to increase revenue. Include one bingo card in the price of the ticket.

✓ Host the gathering on a Saturday over lunch to net the most attendees.

✓ Refrain from allowing guests to bring children by emphasizing adults/women only.

At a Glance —	
Event Type:	Bingo luncheon
Gross:	$130,000
Costs:	$30,000
Net Income:	$100,000
Volunteers:	20
Planning:	8 months
Attendees:	400
Revenue Sources:	Ticket sales, silent auction, bingo card sales, raffle, donations
Unique Features:	Large number of prizes; many ways to win

Source: Mary Blake Meadows, DCAC League Member and former Event Chair, Dallas Children's Advocacy Center, Dallas, TX. Phone (214) 818-2600. E-mail: chuckandmbbmeadows@att.net

Make Your Fundraising Fashion Show a Runway Success

Hosting a successful fashion show fundraiser has its challenges. Offering its 5th annual Young Women's Alliance Foundation Fashion Show (Austin, TX), the organization drew 300 guests, raised $10,000 and overcame any obstacles with style.

Angela Pedowitz, vice president of marketing for the organization that enriches, empowers and educates young Central Texas women, answers questions about creating this memorable event filled with fashion, fundraising and friendraising opportunities:

What are your best suggestions for finding a venue for a fashion show fundraiser?

"Our biggest obstacle was finding a space that could accommodate a runway and 300 people and still fit in our budget. To maximize our fundraising effort, we wanted a venue willing to host our event at little to no cost. Location was also a consideration — our target demographic spends a lot of time in the downtown area, so we knew that's where we wanted to host the fashion show. We found the right combination at the Parish — a local nightclub."

How do you go about coordinating the fashion — do local designers contribute, and if so, how do you approach/connect with them?

"A fashion show committee member called local boutiques and scheduled appointments to speak with the owners. She presented them with a packet outlining event details (date, location, expected attendance, etc.) and the number of looks we hoped to have on the runway. Most saw it as a great way to promote themselves to their target demographic — young, stylish Austin women. We found several boutiques that were receptive to donating clothing for the night, and they even helped us promote the event in their stores."

What are your top tips for a successful fashion show fundraiser?

✓ "Start early! Getting commitments from food and beverage sponsors can be difficult.

✓ "Use the media and social media to your advantage. Get your members and supporters to spread the word via Twitter, Facebook and their personal blogs. Don't forget to send a press release and photos after the event to promote your success!

✓ "Ask your friends for help.

✓ "Know that things will go wrong, and plan for them. Overestimate the number of people you're expecting; it's much harder to get additional staff, food and beverages at the last minute."

Source: Angela Pedowitz, Vice President of Marketing, Young Women's Alliance, Austin, TX. Phone (512) 553-6176. E-mail: marketing@youngwomensalliance.org. Website: www.youngwomensalliance.org

Fashion Show Draws Hundreds, Involves Community

For 57 years, the Salvation Army Women's Auxiliary of Peoria, IL, has put on one of the most successful fashion shows in the Midwest. In October 2009, more than 150 models came down the runway in style, donning fashions from stores within the Peoria area.

Major Sharon Smith, divisional director of women's ministries, explains the success of the show and offers tips for putting on a great used-fashion event:

Some 750 people attended this fashion show. Who is invited and how do you draw such high numbers of guests?

"Each store is encouraged to invite folks, auxiliary members fill tables with their friends and colleagues and the Women's Auxiliary also coordinates publicity through the local media to attract guests to one of their two shows."

How much was raised at the last event?

"The event raised $78,000, $65,000 of which was donated as a lead gift for our annual Christmas campaign. The remainder is used for specific program areas at the Salvation Army as well."

What unique aspects of this event create interest?

"The stores themselves are involved with many store managers even modeling their own fashions. Additionally, local celebrity models are sought out, including local sports celebrities, local television anchors and recognizable business folks. It is a fun and anticipated event each year and the consistency of stores and participants is a staple as well."

How many volunteers do you need to put on this event?

"The entire 30-person Women's Auxiliary is involved each year, and many of their family members as well. All of the models are volunteers, so the total number of volunteers is close to 150 each year or more."

What are three great tips for putting on a successful fashion show?

1. "Getting good participation from a variety of stores to include fashions from bridal wear, contemporary fashions, men's, women's and children's clothing.

2. "Dedicated group of employees and volunteers are needed. All 30 members of the Women's Auxiliary have roles to play, whether it's getting stores involved, organizing models, writing the emcee's script, scheduling the venue, choosing the meal, selling ads for the booklet, soliciting underwriting or other aspects of the show.

3. "Attention to detail. As soon as this year's event was over, the process began on next year's event. The incoming chairperson reviews the previous year to see where they need to perhaps strengthen or change things and gets her committee chairs going with meetings and laying the groundwork for the next show. The Women's Auxiliary takes great pride in this annual effort and their lead gift is the largest individual gift we receive each Christmas!"

Rich Draeger, assistant development director, echoes the value of the fashion show, in terms of raising funds, awareness and passion for the organization's cause.

"As a fundraiser, I can honestly say that I have learned things that I can apply to my various endeavors as well from the Women's Auxiliary," Draeger says. "The time and energy and passion they devote to this annual event are staggering and commendable. They are a big reason that The Salvation Army is so well thought of and respected in central Illinois."

Source: Major Sharon Smith, Divisional Director of Women's Ministries; Rich Draeger, Assistant Development Director, Salvation Army Heartland Division, Peoria, IL.
Phone (309) 655-1348.
E-mail: Rich_Draeger@usc.salvationarmy.org.

> *"All 30 members of the Women's Auxiliary have roles to play, whether it's getting stores involved, organizing models, writing the emcee's script, scheduling the venue, choosing the meal, selling ads for the booklet, soliciting underwriting or other aspects of the show."*

Best Ever Directory of Special Events, Fifth Edition.
Edited by Scott C. Stevenson.
© 2010 Stevenson, Inc. Published 2010 by Stevenson, Inc.

There's a reason why galas are among the most popular fundraising events: people enjoy attending them and they can be highly profitable. The challenge is to make your gala distinct from all others — including features that will draw guests back year after year.

Elegant Venue Sets Stage for Grand Event

Consider sprucing up a local estate or underutilized landmark to add elegant style to your next high-end event.

For the second annual wine-tasting for M-ARK Project Inc. (Margaretville, NY), organizers chose a unique, appealing venue: an historic estate — and former home of a descendent of a signer of the Declaration of Independence built in the early 20th Century.

The Broadlands Estate (Andes, NY), had not been used for more than 30 years, making hiring a professional cleaning service the first order of business, says Iris Mead, M-ARK Project Inc. resource development specialist.

"We knew that holding our event at this location would draw a large crowd because it had not been open to the public except for an auction in 1992, and we were not disappointed," says Mead.

Paying $75 each, the event's 188 guests enjoyed a wine and ale tasting along with chamber music and elegant hors d'oeuvres.

Guests sampled wines and ales in a tasting tent on the estate's front lawn and enjoyed more intimate settings at small tables sprinkled about the lawn, where they could sit and enjoy their drinks and hors d'oeuvres.

Inside the mansion, fresh flowers, candles and linens decorated tables as event goers participated in live and silent auctions. Auction items included massages, bed and breakfast stays, ski lift tickets and dining at New York's Russian Tea Room.

A local historian took guests on tours of the historic mansion.

Following the elegant mansion theme, the hearty hors d'oeuvre fare included poached salmon, tea sandwiches, fresh fruit platters, seared filet of beef and more — all at the reasonable cost of $18.50 per guest.

Mead says they were able to keep expenses under control thanks to the generous donations of sponsors and cost breaks by vendors. A local liquor distributor provided the wine, while the ales were donated by a Belgian brewery based in Cooperstown, NY.

Local liquor store owners acted as the professional wine pourers and the brewery generously donated four types of ale and tasting glasses.

"I work with local suppliers who know the work our organization does and tend to give us breaks," says Mead. "I also ask our board members to use their contacts when they can."

Mead kept costs in check wherever possible. She mailed about 500 invitations at the cost of $462, including postage. Cost of paper plates, forks, tables, chairs, linens and rented wine glasses totaled $112. Both the tent rental and portable toilet companies gave cost breaks, charging $100 each.

Source: Iris M. Mead, Resource and Development Specialist, M-ARK Project, Inc., Margaretville, NY. Phone (845) 586-3500. E-mail: iris@markproject.org

At a Glance —	
Event Type:	Wine and ale tasting
Gross:	$22,145
Costs:	$6,973
Net Income:	$15,172
Planning:	2.5 months
Volunteers:	16
Attendees:	188
Revenue Sources:	Ticket sales, live and silent auctions, vendor cost breaks, sponsorships
Unique Feature:	A mansion estate closed for years was opened just for the event

Celebrating 50 Years

To celebrate 50 years in the field of scientific research, the Children's Hospital Oakland Research Institute (CHORI) of Oakland, CA, hosted a gala in October 2009 at the Chabot Space & Science Center (Oakland, CA). Jessika Diamond, interim special events manager, answers questions about the crowd-pleasing event:

Why was the venue of the Chabot Space & Science Center chosen for the event?

"Holding our party in a venue dedicated to science and education was a natural fit. The event began with scientific talks, furthering the theme."

What was unique about the gala?

"Our event was interactive — the reception took place just outside the Beyond Blastoff: Surviving in Space exhibit and we have pictures of guests trying out the interactive exhibits."

How else are you celebrating?

"We held a symposium in March 2010 at CHORI, featuring luminaries in related fields, including genetics, immunobiology, cancer and more discussing the latest discoveries and trends in their fields. Since no celebration of the past and present is complete without looking forward, we included talks and poster presentations from the young researchers at CHORI, the fellows and post-docs."

What tips can you share for marking a significant milestone at an organization?

"Use a milestone anniversary as an opportunity for a fundraising campaign.... Also, use this opportunity to blow your organization's horn about what's been accomplished over time."

Source: Jessika Diamond, Special Events Manager (Interim), Children's Hospital & Research Center Foundation, Oakland, CA. Phone (510) 428-3885. E-mail: Jdiamond@mail.cho.org.

Tips for Gala Success Will Make You Believe in Magic

When your guests tell others about your special event, you hope they will praise the amazing food, awesome speaker and stellar entertainment. But above all, you hope your guests will remember — and share — how the event made a difference in peoples' lives.

Organizers of the Wish Night annual gala for Make-A-Wish Foundation of North Texas (Irving, TX) make sure attendees remember what the event is all about by focusing all aspects on the organization's mission of fulfilling wishes for seriously ill children, says Erin Michel, development director-central region.

"We don't pay for outside entertainment," Michel says. "Our wish kids share their experiences and do an original performance based on the event's theme. You leave knowing exactly what you were there for."

The event has netted more than $7 million since 1997, Michel says, noting factors that contribute to its success:

❑ **A strong and organized volunteer committee.** "This is the bread and butter of the event. We have about 30 people, including a ball chair, broken down in several smaller committees," each with a co-chair who rotates into the chair in subsequent years.

❑ **A dedicated staff person.** A staff person whose sole function is the annual gala gives volunteers consistent support.

❑ **Show-stopping auction items and a superb auctioneer.** "It's really important to think outside the box about what is going to be a stellar item for auctions," says Michel. Some of this year's items include more than $100,000 in diamonds thanks to the Zale Corporation, a sleep-over in Nastia Liukin's gym and a VIP experience with the Dallas Mavericks.

❑ **Building up excitement.** At least two additional events lead up to the annual gala, including a kickoff party and auction preview party, along with a formal check presentation about one month after the event. These provide multiple opportunities to increase visibility, generate media excitement and involve constituents.

Source: Erin Michel, Development Director-Central Region, Make-A-Wish Foundation of North Texas, Irving, TX. Phone (214) 496-5012. E-mail: emichel@northtexaswish.org

At a Glance —	
Event Type:	Black-tie gala
Gross:	$1,259,152
Costs:	$233,929
Net Income:	$1,025,223
Volunteers:	200-plus
Planning:	12 months
Attendees:	1,100
Revenue Sources:	Ticket sales, sponsorships, live and silent auctions, raffle
Unique Feature:	Show-stopping auction items such as a VIP experience with a professional basketball team

Targeted Committees Make Event Successful

Numbers from the Make-A-Wish Foundation of North Texas (Irving, TX) Wish Night are mind boggling: Some 1,110 people attend the event organized primarily by 200 volunteers, with 100 sponsors and 800 auction items.

This recipe has raised more than $7 million in 12 years.

The key ingredient to the event's success? Volunteers.

Thirty volunteers serve on eight committees with 15 subcommittees, handling everything from décor to sponsor asks to catering and marketing, breaking the major event into manageable steps, says Erin Michel, development director-central region.

To structure event-planning committees, Michel says:

✓ **Be specific.** Have job descriptions that include responsibilities prior to, during and after event. Include all the jobs that no one wants to do but that have to get done (e.g., cleaning auction items the night of the event, transporting items back to the office, etc.). Include details that are taken for granted, leaving no room for error (e.g., who does each person report to, what meetings are they required to attend, what records are they expected to keep).

✓ **Have a succession plan.** Why start from scratch every year? Make sure most folks signing on are interested in a multiple-year commitment. Make sure every committee has co-chairs to rotate in to the chair position over the next two years, giving you three year's of stability. This allows you to focus on growing the event, not just finding warm bodies.

✓ **Keep detailed records.** Require all committee chairs and co-chairs to keep detailed records of their activities, functions and any tips.

Breakfast Galas Boost Fundraising, Recruitment Efforts

Prospective donors and volunteers have a deluge of gala dinners, walkathons, auctions and similar events to choose from when deciding where to give their time, money and attention.

To stand out from that pack, consider organizing a breakfast gala.

When staff of the Capital Breast Care Center (CBCC), a community health center in Washington, D.C., began brainstorming its first-ever large fundraising event, "We opted not to go with an evening event, because in my opinion there are just so many of them," says Beth Beck, executive director. "Very few do breakfast events, so we could be unique in that way."

The CBCC's annual breakfast gala raised $50,000 the first year and $100,000 in both its second and third years.

In addition to being a unique event to put on one's social calendar, there are two additional ways that a breakfast gala may be a better choice than other types of fundraising events, Beck says:

❏ **Guaranteed time commitment for guests.** As opposed to dinner receptions — which have the reputation of going on too long because of entertainment or an over-extended cocktail hour — a breakfast gala, by its very nature, will be run on a tight schedule. It promotes a warm yet get-down-to-business ambiance, Beck says. The CBCC's breakfast gala lasts exactly one hour. Because it sticks to its schedule, attendees are pleased with the event and are more likely to return the following year, bringing along more of their friends, family and community members as prospective donors. Beck says attendance at the CBCC's breakfast has increased each year by about 100 people.

❏ **Guaranteed time period for planning purposes.** Because the event does not run over schedule, the event leaders hold the attention of the attendees throughout the program. Therefore, when the CBCC plans its breakfast, it can build up attention over the course of the hour, rather than worry about losing people's attention. "Right before our ask at the end of the event, we show a video in which a woman speaks about the care she received at the center. It creates a personal connection and allows people to really understand what the center does. Even though the video comes at the end of the event, it is the most powerful moment."

Beth Beck, Executive Director, Capital Breast Care Center, Washington, D.C. Phone (202) 870-1139. E-mail: info@capitalbreastcare.org.

Authors Mingle With Guests at Library Fundraiser

Authors were on the move — literally — at the annual fundraiser for the Sacramento Public Library Foundation (Sacramento, CA).

In March 2009, the foundation hosted its seventh Authors on the Move gala. As guests enjoyed a gourmet dinner, they had opportunity to visit with local and regional authors.

April Butcher, executive director, says the 40 participating authors moved from table to table mingling with guests, rotating after spending 15 to 20 minutes at a table.

"The appeal of the event is definitely the authors," Butcher says. "Guests get to talk to the authors, and they have a good time doing it."

Participating authors also enjoyed the opportunity to promote and sell their books. Authors each had a table where guests could visit with them, purchase books and ask them to sign their books. Staff with the Borders bookstore chain coordinated the sale of the books.

The $200 tickets to the event included two keynote speakers (both authors), a raffle and live auction. Sponsorships ranged from $1,500 to $5,000.

Butcher offers advice for organizations interested in hosting a similar event:

✓ Be aware of what giving levels you are attracting. "Only do it if you want to build your donor base at the levels you expect people to give at to either buy the tickets or spend in the auction," she says.

✓ Secure volunteer support.

✓ Make the event fun and appealing to a broad audience. "Don't make decisions solely on your likes and dislikes," Butcher says. "Many people are vulnerable to decision making that way, but it is important to mix in all of the likes and dislikes both for buy-in and for a broader appeal."

At a Glance —	
Event Type:	Gala
Gross:	$120,000
Costs:	$37,000
Net Income:	$83,000
Volunteers:	25
Planning:	400 to 500 hours
Attendees:	360
Revenue Sources:	Ticket sales, sponsorships, live auction, raffle and advertising
Unique Feature:	Authors visit with guests

Source: April Butcher, Executive Director, Sacramento Public Library Foundation, Sacramento, CA. Phone (916) 264-2990. E-mail: abutcher@saclibrary.org

Raise Funds by Becoming 'Stranger Than Fiction'

How did staff at the St. Louis Public Library Foundation (St. Louis, MO) draw some 600 guests and raise $179,000 with its Stranger Than Fiction fundraiser?

Variety, variety and more variety, says Elizabeth Reeves, director of development and communication. "A belly dancer, a didgeridoo player, an escape artist, 15 marionettes and 30 volunteers costumed as literary characters," Reeves says, listing the event's fiction-related attractions. "Oh, and a 30-person gospel choir. Can't forget that."

The event, in the marbled halls of St. Louis's Central Library, played on five categories of fiction: science fiction, mystery, romance, children's literature and banned books.

Caterers worked with foundation staff to create food stations filled with bookishly themed heavy appetizers: 20,000 Leagues Under the Sea-style nautilus sub sandwiches and squid ink pasta with mozzarella pearls filled the science fiction station. Huckleberry Finn tarts and Lady Chatterly's Lover chocolate ganache were among the desserts of the banned books station.

Specifically, she says, organizers and participants played up the literary theme by:

✓ **Dressing the part.** Guests and staff were encouraged to come dressed as their favorite literary characters. "People really went all out," says Reeves. "The costume-party feel added a lot to the atmosphere of the evening."

✓ **Spotlighting literary themes.** Five of the library's outer rooms were decorated for five genres of literature: mystery, romance, sci-fi, banned books and children's literature. The themes continued...

- **In the drink** — A local hotel donated creative drink recipes for the cash bar: "Scarlet Letter Lemonade" and "A Oliver's Martini, with a Twist".

- **In the entertainment** — Thematically appropriate performers were hired for each room: a marionette puppeteer in the children's literature room, an escape artist in the mystery room.

✓ **Featuring a musical interlude.** A full-sized gospel choir filled the historic, high-ceilinged marble room with music. "We wanted to remind people that we have a large collection of sheet music, scores and CDs for checkout," says Reeves.

✓ **Offering a Bookworm's Raffle.** Young volunteers went around selling raffle tickets for a unique literary privilege: to have your name used in a new book by one of several well-known authors.

✓ **Sponsoring a Shh-Silent Auction.** Including signed books, author appearances at your book club and one of 14 sets of customized Build-a-Bear Workshop plush critters, dressed to look like literary characters.

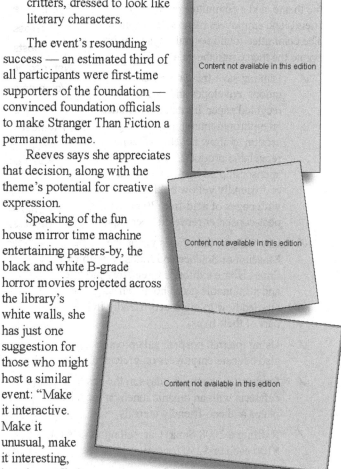

The event's resounding success — an estimated third of all participants were first-time supporters of the foundation — convinced foundation officials to make Stranger Than Fiction a permanent theme.

Reeves says she appreciates that decision, along with the theme's potential for creative expression.

Speaking of the fun house mirror time machine entertaining passers-by, the black and white B-grade horror movies projected across the library's white walls, she has just one suggestion for those who might host a similar event: "Make it interactive. Make it unusual, make it interesting, but above all else, make it interactive. If people are involved, they'll love it."

Source: Elizabeth Reeves, Director of Development and Communication, St. Louis Public Library Foundation, St. Louis, MO. Phone (314) 340-2403. E-mail: ereeves@slplfoundation.org

Promotional materials for the Stranger Than Fiction fundraiser for St. Louis Public Library Foundation (St. Louis, MO) feature fictional characters and a simple, clean invitation

'Green' Theme Incorporated Into Several Event Aspects

Catch the wave of the latest trend and watch even your long-standing event draw in new support.

Officials with Swedish Covenant Hospital (Chicago, IL) capitalized on the environmental movement for the hospital's 53rd annual benefit gala's theme: Going Green.

Amy Fleming, manager of special events and communication in the hospital's foundation office, says the CEO, executive staff and gala chairs developed the theme, and a committee of physicians, friends and employees planned the event. The committee found several ways to incorporate the theme into the gala:

✓ Printing save-the-date cards, invitations, envelopes and inserts on recycled paper. Invitations included an environmental impact savings section to show benefits of using recyclable products. The program/sponsorship ad book cover used eco-friendly yellow birch wood, with pages of acid-free, 30 percent post-consumer recycled fiber paper.

✓ Choosing as the event's venue the Museum of Science and Industry, with its Smart Home exhibit, a three-story module and sustainable green home where guests learned how to make eco-friendly living part of their lives.

✓ Using internal hospital gala promotions to also educate employees on greener choices.

✓ Promoting Organic Fridays in the hospital cafeteria with an organic lunch on recyclable plates and eco-friendly utensils.

✓ Raffling a 2008 Smart Car, selling tickets for $100 each or $250 for three.

✓ Sending employees a bi-weekly e-newsletter highlighting eco-friendly changes in and around the hospital and giving readers tips on how they could go green.

✓ Offering online registrations, and prominently displaying this information on invitations, providing an easier format and saving paper and postage.

✓ Providing guests with eco-friendly insulated shopping bags as parting gifts.

✓ Selecting as that year's recipient of the Spirit of Compassion award a local philanthropist who raised awareness of global warming solutions by founding a Cool Globes exhibit that premiered in Chicago in 2007.

Source: Amy Fleming, Manager of Special Events and Communication, Foundation Office, Swedish Covenant Hospital, Chicago, IL. Phone (773) 878-8200, ext. 2492. E-mail: afleming@schosp.org

At a Glance —	
Event Type:	Gala
Gross:	$668,000
Costs:	$300,000
Net Income:	$368,000
Volunteers:	40
Planning:	8 months
Attendees:	830
Revenue Sources:	Sponsorships, ticket sales, ad book, donations, car auction
Unique Feature:	Theme tied to "Green" movement

Content not available in this edition

Gala Fuels Earth-friendly Moves

Amy Fleming, manager of special events and communication, foundation office, Swedish Covenant Hospital (Chicago, IL) says proceeds from its popular Going Green Gala (detailed at left) are funding environmentally friendly initiatives.

"We announced at the (October 2008) gala and in follow-up letters what projects would be the result of (guests') gifts," says Fleming. Those projects include:

❏ **LED outdoor light conversion.** This pilot project (the first in the city of Chicago) will convert street lighting surrounding the hospital from incandescent to LED bulbs, reducing energy consumption and creating "addressable" street lights, linked to the city's emergency management system, that will blink if 911 is called.

❏ **Parking garage LED light conversion.** Lights in the hospital parking garage will be replaced with energy-efficient LED lamps, reducing energy consumption and electricity cost.

❏ **Cardboard recycling.** Installation of a concrete pad to accommodate a cardboard compactor will enable the hospital to collect and recycle cardboard, reducing waste volume and cost to remove it and generating income, as the hospital is paid per load of cardboard.

University Hosts Leaders in Management Award Dinner

Major annual events can bring awareness and valuable publicity to your mission while connecting you to people capable of providing significant financial support.

Pace University's (New York, NY) 47th Annual Leaders in Management Award Dinner — held April 29 at New York City's Cipriani Wall Street — raised $605,000, says Christine Meola, vice president for philanthropy. Event proceeds, she says, "will count towards Pace's seven-year $100 million Centennial Campaign goal, which we realized two months ahead of schedule."

This year's award recipients were magazine publishing magnate and alumnus David J. Pecker and online advertising innovator Gurbaksh Chahal. Pecker's award was presented by his long-time friend and business associate Donald J. Trump. Bruce Bachenheimer, clinical professor of management, director of entrepreneurship and Wilson Center for Social Entrepreneurship Faculty Fellow, who first made contact with Chahal when he asked him to keynote a university event, presented Chahal's award.

The event attracted 325 people, including Eric Hillman, CEO of Europa Sports Products and an American Media advertiser, who purchased a table and invited celebrities Montel Williams, media celebrity, author, actor, producer, and MS advocate; Elisabeth Hasselbeck, co-host of ABC's "The View" and author of "The G Free Diet"; and Tim Hasselbeck, ESPN NFL analyst and former NFL quarterback to join him.

CNBC Anchor Maria Bartiromo was mistress of ceremonies.

The event, an annual tradition since 1962, celebrates the personal and professional accomplishments of industry and community leaders as well as the university's continued advancement and promising future, says Meola. "It also reunites alums, and showcases our talented musical theater students" who perform at the event.

Tickets for the black-tie event started at $250 (for Young Alumni), and included three other levels — Contributor ($750), Supporter ($1,250) and Sponsor ($2,500), all of which included premium seating and listing in all printed materials.

Sponsor table packages ranged from $10,000 to $50,000. Registration included the option of making a contribution if the person was unable to attend.

The event began with regular and VIP receptions followed by dinner and the awards presentation. Each presenter introduced a video of the honoree's career. For Chahal, they showed an excerpt from his interview with Oprah that included Oprah calling him "one of the youngest and also the wealthiest entrepreneurs on the planet Earth."

To promote the event, Pace distributed a national press release by BusinessWire. Samuella R. Becker, Pace assistant director of public information, says the event "was also featured on online event calendars such as New York Social Diary, Charity Benefits and BizBash Masterplanner, and gossiped about by Rush & Molloy of the NY Daily News. The San Francisco Chronicle also profiled Mr. Chahal in a story that appeared on the front page of one of its sections, entitled 'Internet Star Chahal Getting Honorary Doctorate.'"

Sources: Samuella R. Becker, Assistant Director of Public Information; Christine M. Meola, Vice President for Philanthropy, Pace University, New York, NY. Phone (212) 346-1095 (Becker) or (212) 346-1637 (Meola). E-mail: Sbecker2@pace.edu or cmeola@pace.edu

Walk/run events... golfing events... motorcycle runs... tennis tournaments and more all add an element of excitement and sometimes competition that make a fun time for participants and spectators alike. Outdoor events often draw sought-after publicity.

'Smash Cancer' Tennis Tournament an Ace

Fundraisers such as 5K run/walks flourish across the country and golf tourneys are ubiquitous in mild-weather months.

Tennis tournaments, however, fill an often-overlooked niche, says Peggy Carter, vice president of the Forsyth Medical Center Foundation (Winston-Salem, NC), an organization that hosts an annual tennis doubles benefit.

The foundation's Smash Cancer tennis tournament began in 2005 through the efforts of four community volunteers, all avid tennis players. Since then, it has raised more than $110,000 and drawn consistent participation and sponsorship.

Some 50 players participate in the round robin, pro-set tournament each year. Matched in ability according to the national tennis rating program, two-person teams play five to six matches on their day of play, eventually facing all other teams in their skill grouping.

Though win/loss records are kept for each team, winners are not formally recognized to keep attention on the philanthropic goals of the event, says Carter. This higher aim is reinforced at the two-day event's closing dinner, where total money raised is announced and nurses describe the programs that will receive funding.

The event involves only female players, which Carter says was the result of a gradual process of transition and not a formal decision on the part of organizers, "It was a mixed event for the first several years, but this just seems to fit our supporters," she says, adding that the event has consistently sold out and receives wide acclaim.

For those interested in starting a tennis tournament, Carter recommends collaborating with a committed player or pro first. "Someone who loves tennis and has an affinity for your cause can make all the difference; their impact on the organizing process can't be overstated."

Source: Peggy Carter, Vice President, Forsyth Medical Center Foundation, Winston-Salem, NC. Phone (336) 718-2101. E-mail: Pccarter2@novanthealth.org

Cut Event Costs, Boost Event Proceeds

To make your funding stretch in a tight economy, consider these strategies for your next special event, which Peggy Carter and staff at the Forsyth Medical Center Foundation (Winston-Salem, NC) used to help cut costs of their Smash Cancer tennis tournament by more than a third:

- **Flowers by donation**. Instead of buying professional arrangements from a florist as had been done in past years, staff saved significant money by using only donated blooms.

- **Reusable signage**. Large (5 X 3 feet) poster boards thanking event sponsors were replaced by sturdy sponsor boards staff can use year after year.

- **Dropping shirts**. Printed T-shirts had been included in the registration fee, but, Carter says, "Volunteers told us in tough times they would prefer we drop the shirts and increase the philanthropy."

First-year Golf Tourney Benefits Heart Foundation

Each person touched by tragedy heals in his or her own special way. For most people, having some good come out of the tragedy proves rewarding.

It was this motivation, and a need to honor their daughter, Maggie, who died of heart-related issues at just 14 months of age in July 2008, that drove John and Mollie Stewart to organize the first-ever We Love Maggie Heart Golf Tournament.

The May 24, 2009 event brought in $48,000 for the Children's Heart Foundation of Nevada (Las Vegas, NV). Planning began in December 2008 and involved the nonprofit's full-time development manager, part-time executive director and 18 board members, including the Stewarts.

"The success of this event is attributed to being able to have Mollie act as coordinator and her having her finger on the pulse of all facets of the event at all times," says Renee Rietgraf, foundation development manager.

The tournament, hosted by the Stewarts, drew 175 golfers who paid $125 per person or $400 for a foursome. Black Mountain Country Club reduced green fees and food costs due to the large number of anticipated participants, while extensive networking netted donations of all levels to help expand the tourney's scope.

"We drove to create an incentive for the attendees and to make our event more than just a golf tournament," Rietgraf says. "Having a raffle, silent auction, children's activities and a banquet allowed us to attract additional bidders and banquet attendees and to accomplish our goal. We provided welcome gifts to all 175 golfers, awarded seven golfing groups, handed out approximately 150 raffle items and auctioned off approximately 50 items."

Source: Renee Rietgraf, Development Manager, Children's Heart Foundation of Nevada, Las Vegas, NV 89109. Phone (702) 967-3522. E-mail: Renee@childrensheartcenter.com

New Event Celebrates Olympics, Partners With Other Events

Duluth, MN is home to many past winter Olympians, and the 2010 Snowlympics honored that history by combining two weeks of outdoor snow events with the popular televised 2010 Winter Olympics. The two-week event drew more than 2,500 participants.

Coordinator Barbara Weinstein shares tips for planning two weeks of winter events:

✓ Reach out to event sponsors in your community who currently host popular annual events that will fit nicely with your festival. Weinstein sought out planners from annual events such as Duluth's Warmer by the Lake event to merge with Snowlympics. Warmer by the Lake's family-oriented snow activities, bonfires and hayrides became Snowlympics' opening ceremonies. For closing ceremonies, Snowlympics worked with organizers of the Chester Bowl Winter Carnival and College of Saint Scholastica's Kaleidoscope Multicultural Club fireworks display.

✓ When merging your events with other annual events in your community, be sure to utilize their already established volunteers during your extended event. "AmeriCorps members were an integral part in developing and implementing several events due to the placement of members in the City of Duluth's Park and Recreation locations," says Weinstein. "Without the leadership and creativity of True North AmeriCorps members, the Snowlympics would not have been the success it was."

✓ Merge with other local event planners to find special events that will meet the needs of all community members. Weinstein worked with Courage Duluth — an organization dedicated to persons with physical challenges — to include their Mono-Ski Race within Snowlympics. Courage Duluth's mono-ski camp trains Paralympics hopefuls so including them in the Snowlympics festivities was a natural fit!

✓ Package events to maximize participation and reboot events that have not happened in awhile. At Snowlympics, organizers worked with the Lake Superior Zoo to reinvent the sledding party for the festival. Snowlympics organizers also piggybacked the family-friendly zoo sledding party with free family skating to maximize the number of families that would attend in one day.

✓ Make your event's mission to get attendees to think, "I hope they do this again!" Provide free entertainment, educational opportunities and a blend of great events to get your attendees to want more.

Source: Barbara Weinstein, Event Coordinator, City of Duluth, Duluth, MN. Phone (218) 390-7533. E-mail: info@fitcityduluth.com. Website: www.FitCityDuluth.com

Six High Schools, One Highly Successful Fundraiser

Though the organization was less than a year old, staff and supporters of the United Mount Diablo Athletic Foundation (Concord, CA) knew they couldn't wait to raise funds. Because of the economy, all funding for athletic programs in the East San Francisco Bay Area school district had been eliminated the previous spring, and time was running out for this year's winter sports programs.

"We'd done a couple small fundraisers, but we were scrambling to meet a $200,000 goal," says Pat Middendorf, president of the foundation's executive board. "We knew we needed something big."

A 5K run/walk benefiting all six of the district's high schools turned out to be that big something, raising $102,000 and drawing 2,200 participants.

"Combining the high schools was key," Middendorf says of the turnout that more than doubled expectations. "Friendly rivalry definitely increased student participation, and having them work together drew a huge amount of attention, especially from large businesses and prominent community members."

The high level of interest led to positive publicity and local media attention. Foundation officials distributed fliers, posters and e-mails, while the foundation also benefited from donated newspaper advertising, news coverage and television ads.

And though holding a combined fundraiser meant that all revenue would have to be split six ways — an objection raised by some in the early planning stages — the benefits went well beyond the 5K itself. Middendorf estimates that the foundation received more than $50,000 in direct donations — including two five-figure gifts from community organizations — over the three weeks preceding the event.

At a Glance —	
Event Type:	5K Run/Walk
Gross:	$108,000
Costs:	$6,000
Net Income:	$102,000
Volunteers:	100
Participants:	2,200
Planning:	4 months
Revenue Sources:	Entry fees, student sponsorships, corporate sponsorships
Unique Feature:	Participation of six school districts

Source: Pat Middendorf, President, Executive Board of the United Mount Diablo Athletic Foundation, Concord, CA. E-mail: info@UnitedMTDiabloAthletics.org

Polar Plunge: Take the Plunge to Offer a Special Event

Supporters of Special Olympics Wisconsin (Madison, WI) look forward every winter to the organization's Polar Plunges, in which participants gather pledges to jump into icy lakes.

The popular events have helped raise more than $7 million in 10 years.

This year's plunges combined to raise nearly $1.3 million, with 8,369 people taking frigid plunges at 11 locations across the state: Stevens Point, Pleasant Prairie, Muskego, Oshkosh, Whitewater, Eau Claire, Madison, Green Bay, Wausau, La Crosse and Milwaukee.

In Madison, WI, John Weichelt, regional director of development for Special Olympics Wisconsin, put on a highly successful plunge, bringing together 2,500 participants at Lake Monona. This year's event raised $360,000.

Kloepping suggests tips for putting on a fun-filled, yet safe, plunge in your area:

❑ Match the plunge with other outdoor snow events such as ice bowling, chili cook-off, ice shuffleboard, sledding and such.

❑ Offer a cop-out much like Special Olympics Wisconsin does. Anyone who does not want to brave the waters can be a "chicken" and get the "Too Chicken to Plunge" shirt or hat, while still being able to raise money for the cause. (Each of the 11 locations sponsors its own "Too Chicken to Plunge" events, such as having persons who do not want to get wet do the chicken dance lakeside instead.)

❑ Special Olympics doesn't let Mother Nature stand in the way of the planned event. Instead, they allow a "Big Toe Plunge" or "Pinky Plunge" so that all participants can conform to the plunge rules without necessarily having to do a full-body dip.

❑ Have emergency medical teams and a diving team on hand in the event of an emergency.

❑ Provide heated changing tents for plungers and plenty of warm food and drink.

"The Polar Plunge truly offers individuals a chance to not only support a great cause, but to have some wacky fun with friends and family while doing so," says Kloepping. "We take our hats off to the thousands who have taken the icy dip."

Source: Kelly Kloepping, Vice President of Marketing and Communications, John Weichelt, Regional Director of Development, Special Olympics Wisconsin, Madison, WI. Phone (608) 222-1324. E-mail: kkloepping@specialolympicswisconsin.org

At a Glance —	
Event Type:	Midwinter lake plunge at Madison, WI (one of 11 such events statewide)
Gross:	$370,000
Costs:	$10,000
Net Income:	$360,000
Volunteers:	100
Planning:	6 months, plus state committee meets 10 months prior for early-stage planning
Attendees:	2,500 plungers, 2,500 spectators
Revenue Sources:	Pledges, sponsorships
Unique Features:	Participants seek pledges to jump into frigid lakes; persons can opt out by taking part in "Too Chicken to Plunge" events

Triathlons and Charities Make for a Winning Team

Think participating in a triathlon is a big yet rewarding commitment? Try organizing one.

"Coordinating a triathlon is a lot, a lot of work," says Michelle Kerr, assistant director of special events at the Children's Hospital of Philadelphia (CHOP) Foundation (Philadelphia, PA), the official charity partner of the Philadelphia Insurance Triathlon.

Kerr says that logistics can be so involved that most charities simply partner with an external triathlon. That's what CHOP officials did six years ago when a resident physician put officials in touch with the organizers of the Philadelphia race.

Partnering with a seasoned triathlon presenter doesn't mean a free ride for the foundation, though. Kerr says CHOP staff recruit athletes, donors and fundraisers not only for the full Olympic triathlon, but for a smaller sprint race as well.

"The Karr Barth Charity Challenge, which is part of the Sprint Race, opens the events to a much wider demographic," says Kerr. "You can do it all yourself, but you can also participate as part of a relay team. Having the option to just run or just swim or bicycle is more realistic for a lot of people."

Kerr explains that teams must have at least four individuals, including at least one woman, and that each is encouraged to raise $150 or more. Prizes go to the team finishing with the best combined time, the team raising the largest amount of money and the team with the most members.

Kerr acknowledges that triathlons are more specialized than traditional run/walk fundraisers, but says participants find the race a challenging and rewarding experience.

Charities, she says, find them rewarding, too. Over its six years of participation, CHOP has seen a steady increase in revenue from the triathlon, culminating in a gross of $120,000-plus in the 2009 event.

Source: Michelle Kerr, Assistant Director of Special Events, The Children's Hospital of Philadelphia Foundation, Philadelphia, PA. Phone (267) 426-6517. E-mail kerrm@email.chop.edu

Walk/Race to Remember Raises Funds, Friends

Susan Sanders, head of marketing and public relations at Hospice of Marshall County (Albertville, AL), loves to run. And she loves her job.

So five years ago, she combined both passions into a race that would raise funds and awareness about her organization. Sanders says she knew a 5K race would engage a new demographic of fundraisers while helping people in her community become more aware of the work that the Hospice of Marshall County does.

The Walk/Race to Remember encourages participants to race in honor of a loved one they have lost — thereby strengthening the Hospice of Marshall County's Mission within their community.

Sanders details how she and her colleagues organize this popular, profitable event:

- **What:** A 5K and Fun Run. Sanders wanted to create an event that would attract seasoned and beginning runners alike. She and her planning team made sure to include elements that they enjoyed from races in which they had taken part, such as water stops and having their names called out as they crossed the finish line.

- **Where:** A circuitous route along the streets of their community, reserved well ahead of time with the city, blocked off, and ending at the gymnasium of a local college.

- **When:** 6:30 a.m. until early afternoon, early March. Sanders explains that this is the best time of year to attract people who have made the New Year's resolution to start running, giving them two months to train.

- **How they make their money:** Race participants pay $15 registration fees and are encouraged to use the platform to raise additional gifts for the hospice organization. Additionally, local individuals and companies can pay $500 to $2,000 to have their name or logo printed on all promotional materials.

- **Expenses:** Expenses included official U.S. Track and Field Association staff and equipment to record runners' times, as well as one-time registration fees for online fundraising programs for runners to use in garnering donations. Meanwhile, these items were all donated to benefit the event:
  - ✓ Customizable stickers, for people walking in memory of a loved one.
  - ✓ Food, door prizes and goody bags.
  - ✓ $100 cash prize and trophies for top runners. "We felt this was important," says Sanders, adding, "the 14-year-old girl who won in her age and gender group last year donated the money back to the hospice. For us, it's about encouraging the competitive accomplishment."
  - ✓ Prizes for top-fundraising individuals and groups.
  - ✓ Advertising: ad space, posters and brochures.
  - ✓ Time. Sanders says the event requires a huge number of dedicated volunteers, and that they are fortunate to have local students, churches, and community groups get involved.

- **The Result:** The Walk/Run to Remember is increasingly successful. In 2009, they registered almost 900 runners, to the tune of a $25,000 profit. Sanders says the event has the capacity to raise even more. "We are working on building more support for the participant fundraising efforts," she says, but emphasizes how happy they are with the event so far.

Source: Susan Sanders, Head of Marketing and Public Relations, Hospice of Marshall County, Inc., Albertville, AL. Phone (256) 891-7724. E-mail: info@hospicemc.org or ssanders@hospicemc.org.

Hospital Foundation Reels in Support at Fishing Fundraiser

When River Hospital (Alexandria Bay, NY) opened in 2004, Jeanne Snow, event organizer says many organizations offered to help raise funds. One organization that has been a mainstay is the Alexandria Bay Fishing Guides Association.

For the past six years, the association has hosted A Day with a Fishing Guide, a fundraiser for the hospital that has raised more than $43,000 to date.

For the event, held the Sunday of Memorial Day weekend, local anglers (usually four per boat) pay $140 each to be paired with fishing guides. The guides donate the use of their boats, time and expertise.

Fishing parties are given their respective guides' names at the Alexandria Bay village dock. Parties leave the docks at 8 a.m., arriving at the Thousand Islands Bridge Authority's Wildlife Refuge Preserve around noon after a morning of guided fishing.

At the preserve, fishing parties are treated to a shore dinner, coordinated by a fishing guide's wife, who does all of the shopping and takes all the needed supplies to the refuge. Participants snack on appetizers while the volunteers clean and cook the day's catch, served with salt potatoes, tossed salad and Texas toast.

Snow herself is a volunteer and helps coordinate the whole event, overseeing all of the other volunteers. Snow says volunteers are a huge part of the success.

As a thank-you and to remind participants about the philanthropic nature of the day's fishing, River Hospital Foundation provides specialized, brimmed caps for the anglers, guides and volunteers, as well as prizes for the boat and captain with the most fish and the angler with the largest fish.

Source: Jeanne Snow, Event Organizer, River Hospital Foundation, Inc., Alexandria Bay, NY. Phone (315) 482-4976. E-mail: jsnow@ridgeviewtel.net

Students Get to Cross Finish Line Thanks to Race

What began as a challenge from a college president to his public relations person to find a fundraiser that wasn't a golf tourney is now one of the largest charity events of its kind.

In its first year, the Texarkana (Texarkana, TX) College Bulldog 100 Mini NASCAR Race raised more than $25,000. Funds benefit the college's Rising Star Scholarship Program. More than $200,000 has been raised for the program from the Bulldog 100 since its inception. Here's how it works:

- Companies purchase go-karts from the college at a cost of $2,750, which includes the entry fee, kart and two helmets. Companies then customize their cars and prepare them to compete — one team even got a $3,500 paint job on their car.

- Race weekend kicks off on Wednesday when the cars parade approximately one mile from the mall — where they have been on display — to the campus.

- On Thursday night there is a pit-stop competition and BBQ banquet for the teams.

- On Friday morning cars are inspected by a 25-person tech team to ensure that all cars are safe, fair and within the race's guidelines. After that, teams compete in qualifying races on a track located right on the college campus.

- Cup races are held on Saturday, with trophies awarded at the end of the day.

Event technical director and former racer Benny Murphy, also an automotive and diesel technology instructor at the school, says the event is labor-intensive but well worth the effort. "As a teacher I get to see the results firsthand. I see students coming to college who wouldn't have been able to otherwise. You just can't limit the value of education, so it's all worth it."

Source: Benny Murphy, Technical Director, Bulldog 100 Mini NASCAR Race, Texarkana College, Texarkana, TX. Phone (903) 832-5565. E-mail: bmurphy@texarkanacollege.edu

Involvement and Value Winning Combination for Race Teams

Consider your event's target audience, then look for ways to engage businesses that seek that audience as well, advises Benny Murphy, technical director for the Texarkana College (Texarkana, TX) Bulldog 100 Mini NASCAR Race.

Murphy says that when he started reaching out to car dealers, auto parts stores and other local businesses to be the first teams to compete in the event, he had no idea how positive the response would be. It was so positive, that he had to order additional cars and limit the number of racing teams to ensure safety and fairness.

Murphy cites two reasons he believes the event resonates with participants:

1. **Value.** Because teams purchase their cars, they are able to use the vehicles for their own promotional and marketing purposes. Murphy says many companies use their cars for advertising, and even ride in them during the local fair parade and Christmas parade. Participation in the race guarantees cars will be seen during the display of cars at the mall for four days prior to the kick-off parade, during the kick-off parade, during the pit-stop competition and during all of the races. Cars are seen by as many as 5,000 people over the course of the event, in addition to the added promotional value for the life of the car.

2. **Community.** Murphy says the race brings companies together as team members work to customize their cars and participate in multiple events. In addition to the races, teams can compete for Best Dressed Team/Pit Crew and Fastest Pit Crew. "Their involvement really becomes personal," Murphy says. "It's more than just a fundraiser. It has really turned into the community's event."

Texarkana College Bulldog Mini 100 Nascar Race by the Numbers

Highest number of people attending race weekend: 3,000 to 5,000 in 2007

Original number of cars racing: 43, based on the number of cars in Daytona 500

Highest number of cars racing: 68 in 2007

Number of volunteers needed: 200-plus

Record number of funds raised in one year: Approximately $88,000 in 2008

Length of time it takes to prepare track: Two weeks

Record time in pit-stop competition: 9.16 seconds

Motorcycle Riders Cruise to Victory in Fundraising Efforts

You might not think that motorcycle riders and sick children go together, but George S. Wilson, one of the organizers of the Cruise Motorcycle Benefit Ride for the Ronald McDonald House (Rochester, MN) says you couldn't be more wrong.

"The riders might look rough in some cases, but they have hearts of gold and would do anything for the kids that are going through treatments and staying at the Ronald McDonald House," Wilson says.

That might explain why the biker-driven event has raised more than $500,000 in the last eight years and grown to become the largest motorcycle benefit ride in southern Minnesota.

A committee of 12 to 15 volunteers begins work 10 months before the annual event to plan the route, solicit donations and make arrangements. They select stops along the 132-mile ride, arrange food at those stops, coordinate a live and silent auction and plan a parade that goes from the ride's end point, Rochester Community College, to the Ronald McDonald House.

The committee also secures the necessary permits for the parade and business sponsors at two different levels: $1,000 and $2,500.

Event day starts very early with 30 to 40 volunteers handling registration, staging the auctions, placing sponsor banners and checking microphones and other equipment to make sure everything is ready for the big day.

Wilson says that the committee changes the route every year to keep interest up among the riders, but that it's really the parade and the chance to meet with the children at the house that keep them coming back.

Following the parade, organizers present an oversized check to children at the Ronald McDonald House.

The 2008 event included 1,237 riders and raised $104,000, helping offset the house's operating budget by 10 percent.

Source: George S. Wilson, Rochester, MN. Phone (507) 288-3834. E-mail: gewilson@heartman-insurance.com

At a Glance —	
Event Type:	Motorcycle benefit ride and parade
Gross:	$110,000-plus
Costs:	$8,000 to 9,000
Net Income:	$100,000-plus
Volunteers:	12 on committee; 30 to 40 more on event day
Planning:	10 months
Attendees:	1,200-plus
Revenue Sources:	Rider registration, sponsorships and T-shirt sales
Unique Feature:	Largest motorcycle benefit ride in southern Minnesota

Chasing Ambulances Helps Victims of Violence

The Ambulance Chase started as a way to turn a negative event into a positive one and ended as a way to raise awareness and funds for the Family Violence Center (Springfield, MO).

The event is coordinated by Phi Alpha Delta Pre-Law Fraternity – Eric Hutson Chapter, Missouri State University (Springfield, MO).

"The concept comes from the way that lawyers are sometimes jokingly called ambulance chasers," says Kelsey Bartlett, a local college student who created the concept and helped bring it to life. "We thought we would redirect the negative connotation into a positive, and create a fun community event for lawyers, students, and the others to attend at the same time."

During the event, budding lawyers chase a Cox EMS ambulance one mile to a finish line in front of the Federal Courthouse.

Runners pay $10 to register and receive an event T-shirt that lists all of those who have donated to the Family Violence Center. Runners wear the shirts during the event and secure sponsorships from local law firms. Bartlett says that connection is an added perk for prospective runners. "Reaching out to local law firms is a

great way for future lawyers to make connections to secure internships and employment, while helping a great charity."

While the 2010 inaugural event ran into some roadblocks — trying to secure an ambulance to chase, as well as permits and clearances, at the last minute — Bartlett says she is hopeful that the event laid the groundwork for a successful annual event. That would allow the event's leaders to focus more on fundraising alone, which would help shelter staff continue to make the shelter a warm, encouraging place for victims to turn into success stories instead of statistics.

Source: Kelsey Bartlett, Chairperson, Special Events Committee, Phi Alpha Delta Pre-Law Fraternity – Eric Hutson Chapter, Missouri State University, Springfield, MO. Phone (417) 294-7965. E-mail: Kelsey3@live.missouristate.edu

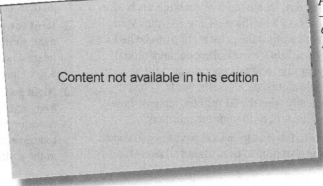
Content not available in this edition

Implementing Changes at Golf Tournament Improves Event

Just as knocking a stroke or two off of your golf game can make a major difference in your links experience, knocking out a few new, crowd-pleasing elements for your golf-themed fundraiser can help you draw more people and boost the event's bottom line.

For six years, Kaplan University (Fort Lauderdale, FL) has organized a successful golf tournament, which this year raised $30,000 for three South Florida nonprofits.

Sherry Thompson, manager of events and community outreach for Kaplan Higher Education, explains some changes they implemented for the 2010 event:

What new elements did you introduce to the event this year?

"For its sixth annual charity golf tournament, Kaplan University asked attendees to complete a survey providing feedback about the tournament. In exchange for the completed survey card, they were entered into a raffle drawing for a chance to win a prize. For the first time, Kaplan University event officials also used two-way radios to communicate with the director of the tournament, key volunteers and those at the registration tables."

What changes did you make this year to accommodate volunteer management?

"Kaplan University recruited more than 40 volunteers to manage the courses. Kaplan organizers hosted an orientation for volunteers three days before the tournament and gave the volunteers directions, a written timeline, contact information and a list of items to bring on the day of the tournament. Volunteers were pre-assigned duties and received their tasks the day of the event, along with a 30-minute briefing to make sure duties were clear.

"Also new this year, Kaplan University created a volunteer check-in table where volunteers signed in, received their event shirt and assignment. This worked well, as they had a designated space to check in, obtain information and to check out. All volunteers were provided an event shirt, differentiating them from the players."

Any snags that you had to overcome? If so, what? How were they handled?

"As a result of Kaplan University's increased player participation (244 golfers), event officials needed to use two separate dining rooms in the same clubhouse for its post-tournament awards banquet. For all participants to see and hear the awards and presentation of proceeds to the benefiting organizations, the presentation was held in one room while Kaplan University officials used audio/video equipment to broadcast to the second room.

One snag encountered during the planning process was the amount of time it took for a winner announced in room A to exit and enter room B. To accommodate this, Kaplan University used two volunteers to serve as a runner and a spotter. The spotter signaled the winner in room A, and the runner took the award and met the winner upon entering room B. This helped keep the awards banquet on schedule."

Sources: Sherry Thompson, Manager of Events and Community Outreach; Linnea Brown, Senior Public Relations Associate, Kaplan University, Fort Lauderdale, FL. Phone (954) 515-3651. E-mail: LBrown3@kaplan.edu. Website: www.kaplan.edu/talent

Five Ways to Increase Your Golf Event Revenue

You've sold 18 holes of corporate sponsorship opportunities, collected dozens of pledge forms, and prepared a raft of mulligans to sell to well-heeled duffers.

Looking for more ways to leverage your golf fundraiser and raise the maximum funds for your cause? Consider these creative, lesser-known strategies:

❑ **Million-dollar shootout**. Start with a pocketbook friendly $3 to $5 closest-to-the-pin contest on any par 3 hole. Record distances throughout the event, and at the end of the day, let the top five qualifiers each take their shot at a cool $1 million on any 165-plus yard hole. Insurance against the prize money can be had for under $200 (see http://www.holeinoneinternational.com for one option) and this opportunity will be sure to keep people around to watch the finale. (Plus, if someone actually wins the $1 million, imagine how generous he/she will be to your organization!).

❑ **Beat the pro**. In this strategy, a local pro willing to donate his or her time goes head-to-head against all takers for bets of up to $50 (or whatever limit you choose). If the pro ends closer to the pin on a single drive, the player loses his/her money. If the player edges out the pro, he/she doubles the money. A good pro can generate significant money over the course of an afternoon.

❑ **Mini-golf**. Widen the age appeal of your event with a family friendly mini-golf challenge held concurrently with the main tournament. Selling sponsorship opportunities and asking younger golfers to collect pledges can add significant revenue.

❑ **Rent the pro**. Everyone needs a little help now and then, so let them buy it! Station pros at several of the longest holes on the course and let players pay $10 to $50 to hire a professional drive from the tee box.

❑ **Night golf**. Attract players and distinguish your event from others through the novelty of nighttime golf. A nocturnal showdown can supplement the primary tournament or be the main event, but be sure to use glow-in-the-dark balls and aim for a night with a full moon.

Hike-a-thon Connects Contributors With Services

Nonprofits often stage fundraisers that, while successful, have little to do with their mission. Not so for the second annual People for Trails Hike-a-thon, which raised more than $13,000 by sending people out on the very trails their contributions would support.

"It was fundraising, but it was education and outreach as well," says Jennifer Hezel, development associate of the New York-New Jersey Trail Conference (NYNJTC), Mahwah, NJ, an organization dedicated to creating, protecting and maintaining more than 1,700 miles of hiking trails. "It was about connecting people to the beauty of this area and showcasing the work our volunteers do throughout the year."

Staged at Bear Mountain State Park, the hike-a-thon drew 60 participants to four predetermined routes ranging from three to 12 miles. All participants committed to a goal of raising at least $200. Top fundraisers received donated prizes such as outdoor apparel, framed nature photographs and sports club memberships.

Outdoor retail vendors and sponsors were also invited to set up display booths at the staging ground, but in keeping with the event's focus on outreach, they provided only information, not merchandise.

Staging the hike-a-thon in only eight short weeks, publicity was crucial, says Hezel. NYNJTC staff relied on e-mail blasts sent to a database of around 40,000 members. They also utilized sponsors' mailings lists, produced a short radio spot and sent postcards and posters to outdoor merchants in the area.

Though onsite registration was available and utilized, Hezel identifies online pledging as a key to the event's success.

Online pledging was very, very helpful, she says. "Though it can be a lot to learn at first, it allows you to know who has raised what in real time, which is a great help in planning." The event management service she used, Dojiggy, not only set up individual pledge pages for participants, but also tracked the number of people registered, the hiking routes they had chosen, and other such details.

Beyond this technology, Hezel also points to the event's spirit — not a race to be won, but a celebration to be shared by outdoor enthusiasts — as central to its appeal.

At a Glance —	
Event Type:	Hike-a-thon
Gross:	$16,000
Costs:	$3,000
Net Income:	$13,000
Volunteers:	10
Planning:	8 weeks
Attendees:	60
Revenue Sources:	Pledges, registration fees, corporate and nonprofit sponsorships
Unique Feature:	Held on the oldest section of the Appalachian Trail

Source: Jennifer Hezel, Development Associate, New York-New Jersey Trail Conference. Mahwah, NJ. Phone (201) 512-9348. E-mail: Hezel@nynjtc.org

Best Ever Directory of Special Events, Fifth Edition.
Edited by Scott C. Stevenson.
© 2010 Stevenson, Inc. Published 2010 by Stevenson, Inc.

Who isn't attracted to food and drink — especially when it's presented creatively or under unique circumstances? Guests' culinary experiences will often be the highlight of an event and will significantly impact their overall perceptions.

Unique Food, Drink Pairings Create a Party in the Mouth

Get people raving about your food and drink and you've got a successful event on your hands. Just ask Stacy LaCombe-Kraft, coordinator of special events and gifts at Seton Health Foundation (Troy, NY), where amazing food and decadent drinks are the rule for the annual Hopscotch & Slide fundraiser.

"Guests are not just eating and drinking," she says, "they are experiencing. When people attend, we want them to be exposed to new and exciting food and drink partnerships that essentially create a party in your mouth."

To accomplish this, organizers place stations throughout the room that pair a culinary style with a specific beverage type. For example, says LaCombe-Kraft, "This year Mansion Catering featured Asian delicacies like Japanese dim sum and sesame Thai chicken skewers with the Martini Slide station. The Absolute Berry Acai martinis were served from an ice sculpture with a built-in luge and the station was decorated like an Asian pagoda."

LaCombe-Kraft says the high-energy atmosphere also appeals to the younger professional crowd they seek to target. They achieve this by immediately surrounding guests with elements that appeal to all of the senses. This year that meant guests stepping off elevators at the venue onto a Hollywood-style red carpet complete with a paparazzi-style photo shoot.

LaCombe-Kraft says the event's success still comes down to having an exceptional event planning committee to help you gain momentum. "Hopscotch & Slide would never happen if we didn't have an incredible team of hand-picked individuals who understand the experience we are trying to create as well as the importance of the cause. Our committee members believe in the Seton Health mission and are dedicated to improving the event year after year so that we are constantly out-doing ourselves.

The event has raised more than $360,000 to benefit Seton Health Pediatrics since 2002 and will celebrate its 10th anniversary in 2011.

Source: Stacy LaCombe-Kraft, Coordinator of Special Events and Gifts, Seton Health Foundation, Troy, NY. Phone (518) 268-5604. E-mail: SLacombe@setonhealth.org

Unique Pairings Also Boost Silent Auction

Stacy LaCombe-Kraft, coordinator of special events and gifts, Seton Health Foundation (Troy, NY) says their annual Hopscotch & Slide event not only benefits from unique pairings of food and signature drinks, but from strategic pairing of auction items as well.

"We spend weeks packaging items together, rearranging, creating bid sheets and inventing attractive displays," she says. "We also pay attention to feedback from guests and do our best to obtain donations that will enhance the packages and appeal to bidders."

The silent auction, which is a significant part of the fundraising evening, typically has more than 50 items, including big-ticket items such as packages with concert tickets and sports memorabilia.

LaCombe-Kraft says the auction is set up in categories so people can stick to the most appealing items, like date night packages which pair restaurants, hotels and show tickets together. This year's big sellers included a flat screen TV and Rock Band Hero combo package, as well as a trip to see "Wicked" on Broadway and an autographed Mickey Mantle photograph.

Singles Event Raises Funds, Possibilities of Romance

How did five friends with no formal background in fundraising raise nearly $6,000 for the Center for Autism Research at the Children's Hospital of Philadelphia (Philadelphia, PA)?

Simple, says Zhanna Davis, founding member of the Philadelphia-based group Singles With a Cause and one of the event's key organizers. Davis says they reached out to a group overlooked in many fundraising events — singles.

"All five of (the founding members) were single and felt that most fundraisers are heavily couples-driven," says Davis. "When we put that together with the fact that people in their 20s have clubs and parties, but people in their 30s and up don't have as many places to meet, we realized that there was a real opportunity to create something unique."

The largely invitation-based event they planned drew 70 participants for an evening of cocktails, hors d'oeuvres and music at an upscale local restaurant. The guests — mostly accomplished professionals ranging in age from early 40s to mid-60s — were treated to a presentation from a representative of the autism center, then given the opportunity to take part in both a raffle and silent auction.

But the biggest attraction for attendees was unquestionably the opportunity to meet and mingle with similar-minded singles, says Davis.

"Raising money for a good cause was always the underlying goal, but the draw, the thing that made the event unique, was the possibility of meeting that somebody special," she explains. "That's what really made people put down $75 for a ticket, and that is what we worked to reinforce through the atmosphere, the music and the invitations."

Source: Zhanna Davis, Cofounder, Singles With a Cause, Levittown, PA 19056. Phone (215) 908-4437. E-mail: Zhannad7@yahoo.com

Back-to-Basics Luncheon Strikes Chord With Donors

Sometimes, pressing the reset button can breathe fresh life into your event.

The Annual Anniversary Luncheon to benefit Providence House (Cleveland, OH) had become tired, says Natalie Leek-Nelson, CEO and president: "Costs were escalating, and we felt the flavor of our organization — a crisis nursery for at-risk children zero to six years old — was lost in the high-end luncheon model. So the organization decided that every change to the event would have to circle back to their mission and the children they serve.

"The results were overwhelming," Leek-Nelson says of the major move. The event raised $20,000 more than it had in the previous year, including $12,000 from the tables alone — an ask that Leek-Nelson says usually garners about $2,000. The following changes left the guests shouting and applauding:

1. **The Menu.** The new menu definitely reflected the children guests were there to support. Guests munched on cut veggies with ranch dressing as their salad, macaroni and cheese as the entrée, and chocolate cake with M&Ms for dessert. Centerpieces of fresh, whole fruit served double duty as guests were encouraged to take their afternoon snack with them as they left the midday event. Leek-Nelson says they are getting suggestions for this year's menu — including grilled cheese and pizza! But what really had guests cheering was the fact that this simple change in menu saved $7,000, which could be put towards the children.

2. **The Ask.** A 10-year-old boy took the podium with his piggy bank, filled with $20 in change. He asked guests to match or beat his $20 gift by passing around a large piggy bank in the center of each table. Each bank was hand-painted and featured photos of Providence House children. During this period he also introduced 10 other children (ages 5 to 12) seated around the room who stood on their chairs to be seen. Each had held fundraisers to help the children at Providence House. This ask raised nearly $12,000 in five minutes.

3. **The Close.** Typically, a video featuring photos of Providence House children is set to music. This year the organization took a leap and did a documentary-style video featuring three mothers telling their stories and one national expert offering perspective on the nursery's model of care.

"The entire event felt focused and had an easier air about it than past luncheons," says Leek-Nelson. "This was about telling our story in a new way — a real way — through real people. From an educational standpoint, it was the first time that we heard attendees say, 'I really get what you do now,' even from some who had attended our events for years. It was back to basics in many ways and refreshing to see that it was a stronger event for it."

Source: Natalie Leek-Nelson, CEO and President, Providence House, Cleveland, OH. Phone (216) 651-5982. E-mail: natalie@provhouse.org

---

Make Event Changes That Reflect Your Mission

 What suggestions do you have for making event changes both smooth and successful?

"Do what makes sense for your organization and be really honest about what you hope to achieve in the changes. In today's economy, every decision must be made to further the highest and best purpose for your organization and your guests. Cutting costs, canceling events or making dramatic changes may make sense as one-offs, but do they make sense in the whole picture of your event? Our changes were dramatic and focused, and each change had a specific reason and response that ultimately circled back to our mission."

— Natalie Leek-Nelson, CEO and President, Providence House (Cleveland, OH)

Fundraiser Hits Sweet Spot

How do members of the Mira Mesa High School Foundation (San Diego, CA) regularly gross $20,000-plus with a single event? Easy. They aim for people's stomachs.

"The Taste of Mira Mesa is a community-wide event showcasing the many ethnic restaurants found in our neighborhood," says Esther Alameddin, foundation president.

Some 15 to 20 restaurants take part every year, donating food and providing the staff to serve it. Though the event is well established now, Alameddin says convincing restaurant owners wasn't hard even the first time. "They see the money spent as an advertising expense," she says. "Some even pass out special coupons to track how much business they create."

Leveraging business connections of another kind, the event is held in the interior courtyard of a local business. Tickets ($25) are sold at the door, but most of the 300-plus tickets are pre-sold to parents, foundation supporters, community members, and students of other area schools.

Student participation is an important key to the event's success, Alameddin says. In the past, the school culinary department provided and served a specially created meal. Currently, student volunteers pass out beverages, help set up and tear down equipment, and provide live music to complement the work of professional disc jockeys and emcees.

"With so many people to coordinate, you need a committee for everything," she says. "Membership, tickets, preparing gift baskets, auctioning off the gift baskets, coordinating restaurants — everything benefits from more hands. But done right, it all leads to a fun and inviting experience."

Source: Esther Alameddin, President, Mira Mesa High School Foundation, San Diego, CA. Phone (858) 692-7662. E-mail: Ealameddin@gmail.com

Empty Bowls to Full Bellies: Event Helps Fund 2 Million Meals

What began as a small fundraising project between a group of Michigan high school students and their art teacher has since grown into Empty Bowls (emptybowls.net), an international project to fight hunger, personalized by artists and art organizations on a community level.

The Empty Bowls event hosted by North Texas Food Bank (Dallas, TX) has raised enough money in its 10-year history to provide 2 million meals, says Sayeda Mahler, cause marketing manager. The idea of the event, she says, is for people to enjoy a simple meal of soup and bread while learning about the need to help feed the community's hungry.

Guests enjoy food from 20 area restaurants and pick a handcrafted bowl to take home as a reminder of helping to feed hungry people.

"Potters, wood turners and art students come together to lend their talent to create beautiful bowls, while chefs prepare amazing soups, bread and desserts to create a one-of-a-kind experience for guests," Mahler says. "People leave with a beautiful handcrafted bowl and a full stomach, knowing they have put food on the table of those in need. All proceeds directly benefit hunger relief."

Mahler says the event is a success for many reasons, including its appeal to such a large audience (e.g., school children, college students and senior citizens) and its venue, the Meyerson Symphony Center.

Perhaps most important is the food bank's relationship with John and Darlene Williams, the founders of the Dallas chapter of Empty Bowls. John is a potter and owner of a ceramic supply store who recruits all of the potters and wood turners, says Mahler. "It's because of their vision that we have such a successful event."

For the event, 1,350 people paid $30 in advance or $35 each at the door to attend, raising more than $146,000.

Source: Sayeda Mahler, Cause Marketing Manager, North Texas Food Bank, Dallas, TX. Phone (214) 347-9579. E-mail: sayeda@NTFB.org

At a Glance —

Event Type:	Simple meal to raise awareness and funds for hunger issues
Gross:	$154,000
Costs:	$8,000
Net Income:	$146,000
Volunteers:	40 day of event; hundreds of potters and wood turners create bowls in advance of event
Planning:	5 months
Attendees:	1,350
Revenue Sources:	Ticket sales, sponsorships, reserved table sales, centerpiece sales, additional bowl sales, bowl auction revenue and People's Choice Award revenue

Content not available in this edition

Food-themed Fundraisers Tap Into Today's Trends

Does it sometimes seem like Food Network is everyone's favorite channel? That's probably because good cuisine has made its way into everyone's consciousness. Why not use this to your advantage and plan a fundraiser around great food?

Theatre Action Project (TAP), Austin, TX — a nonprofit organization that teaches children about social issues and self-esteem through educational theater projects — held its first smackdown-style, food-centric fundraiser in October 2009. Organizers invited celebrity chefs to present their best takes on macaroni and cheese to judges and attendees.

While the event did not include theater-related activities, it still offered a child-inspired environment in line with the organization's spirit, says Liz Kelley, marketing manager. "We actually came up with the idea based on our daily interactions with kids. We know the majority of kids are always up for mac and cheese!"

A food-themed fundraiser works whether it black-tie or family-friendly, Kelly says, noting that even mac and cheese can be made up fancy. (Ever heard of lobster mac and cheese?)

Also, every city has celebrity chefs who can prepare fare at low or no cost to your organization and whose names will draw in attendees.

And while such an event is focused on food, it need not require providing or paying for full meals for every attendee — just a few bites of the competing dishes.

TAP's fundraiser brought in more than 2,000 attendees. With a low, $5 suggested donation, says Kelly, organizers are already planning next year's smackdown: chocolate chip cookies!

Karen LaShelle, Executive and Artistic Director, Theatre Action Project, Austin, TX. Phone (512) 442-8773. E-mail: karen@theatreactionproject.org

Awards Ceremony Honors Heroes of All Breeds

Staff and supporters at the Oregon Humane Society (Portland, OR) have found a winning pedigree when it comes to donor events. The Humane Society's Diamond Collar Awards night honors community members — human and animal alike — who have made significant contributions to the community.

Rachel Good, Humane Society development associate, shares insight into what made the most recent ceremony such a success:

✓ **Lunch timing.** This year they moved the event from a seated dinner to a luncheon slot, which was more suited to people's schedules than an evening event, says Good. She adds that a lunchtime event is less expensive than an evening event.

✓ **A Hero's Celebration.** The ceremony's overall purpose is to celebrate animals and people in the community, says Good, "which means it's not directly about us as an organization." She says this format helps guests look at the Humane Society's work in a larger context, which inspires the spirit of giving more than a typical fundraiser does.

✓ **The Audience.** The ceremony is a "major event for major donors," Good says. An event planning committee works with donor relations and marketing staff to ensure the event's important and inspirational message gets to people who can make the biggest difference.

✓ **The Fundraising:** Event tickets were $55 a seat, while full tables went for $550. Corporate sponsorships ranged from $2,500 to $10,000. A video appeal presented near the ceremony's end took the audience through the Humane Society's accomplishments of the past year, and ended with a breakdown of its programs, during which table captains handed out donation envelopes and encouraged people at their respective tables to make their gifts.

The 2010 Diamond Collar Awards raised more than $70,000, says Good, who is already planning for greater success next year by encouraging competitive donations from attendees and encouraging this year's attendees to bring guests to the 2011 event.

Source: Rachel Good, Development Associate, Oregon Humane Society, Portland, OR. Phone (503) 416-5027. E-mail: rachelg@oregonhumane.org. Website: www.oregonhumane.org

Go Beyond the Norm, Have a Potato Bake

Here's a great alternative to the traditional pancake breakfast: a potato bake.

Get a local restaurant, grocery store or restaurant supply house to donate large potatoes for baking. Try to get the big, one-pound variety. Also, seek in-kind donations or financial gifts to obtain other needed supplies such as aluminum foil, plastic dinnerware, cups, napkins and drinks.

The most important ingredient? Potato toppings. Stock up on specialty items available for stuffing the steaming 'taters, such as the typical topping fare of broccoli and cheese, butter, sour cream, chili, green peppers and onions. Go beyond the norm to add in some fun alternatives: beef stroganoff, grilled onions, jalapenos and such.

Give creative names to the different types of potatoes.

Sell tickets in advance to get a good idea of the number of potatoes required. Start baking the spuds in an oven or grill ahead of the scheduled time and have an area where they can be kept hot as people arrive.

Luncheon Celebrates Women, Raises Funds

The Simi Valley (CA) Hospital Foundation's Hats Off to Women Luncheon celebrates women and all they do in a community, says Debi Schultze, director and chief development officer.

"It is a day for women to focus on taking care of themselves in addition to all they do for their spouses, children, friends and communities."

The event includes a fashion show, keynote speakers, Woman of the Year award and free health screenings, says Schultze.

Education and health outreach are major objectives, but the luncheon is also an effective fundraiser, netting more than $31,000 in 2009.

Revenue is generated through ticket sales and sponsorship, silent and live auctions, and even a boutique shopping pavilion.

Now in its eighth year, the luncheon is popular and well-received, with more than 300 women attending the most recent event, she says. To accommodate steadily growing numbers, the event will move to a new and larger facility next year.

"Everything we do strives to focus on the total well-being of women — on body, mind and spirit," says Schultze of the event's success.

"There are few other opportunities like this, and women really respond to it."

Source: Debi Schultze, Director and Chief Development Officer, Simi Valley Hospital Foundation, Simi Valley, CA. Phone (805) 955-6670. E-mail: Schultd1@ah.org

At a Glance —	
Event Type:	Women's Luncheon Benefit
Gross:	$57,000
Costs:	$26,000
Net Income:	$31,000
Volunteers:	30 to 40
Planning:	5 months
Attendees:	300-plus
Revenue Sources:	Silent and live auctions, ticket sales, boutique, program advertisements, corporate and private sponsorships
Unique Feature:	Holistic focus on women's health and well-being

'Guess What Friend Is Coming to Dinner' Proves Successful for Library

Adding in the element of surprise can help put the special in your next special event.

In 2008, Friends of Florence County Library hosted Guess What Friend Is Coming to Dinner to raise funds for its 2009 Children's Summer Reading Program. The event was such a success, organizers agreed to host the event again in 2009.

Board members determined they could easily reach their goal by:

✓ Promoting an event with reasonable ticket prices to appeal to the public.

✓ Creating an innovative aspect different from what other local nonprofit groups use.

✓ Encouraging participant support in the community by promoting the library as an institution committed to life-long learning.

The idea for the event came from Bob Youngblood, board president. Participants chose from $25 tickets to attend a wine-and-cheese tasting, sponsored by Piggly Wiggly, and have purchased cookbooks signed by well-known cookbook author Nathalie Dupree; or $75 tickets that included all of the above plus a host-sponsored dinner.

Participants at the $75 level received a card at the wine-and-cheese tasting with the name and address of their respective dinner host. Neither guests nor hosts knew who would be attending their dinner until the event night.

The 2009 event raised $6,700 for the library's summer reading program.

Source: Francie Dunlap, Development Officer, Friends of Florence County Library, Florence, SC. Phone (843) 413-7064. E-mail: fhdunlap@gmail.com

Brand Your Special Events With a Signature Cocktail

Today's designer cocktail craze can help add signature style to your special events.

Riya Aarini, director of communications at Roots & Wings International (Spokane, WA), says the organization, which promotes elementary through university education in rural Guatemala, features a signature drink at its Annual Cocktail Reception Benefit. She shares secrets learned when it comes to crafting the right cocktail for your crowd:

✓ The fewer ingredients, the better. On the first venture into creating a signature drink, Aarini says, "We held a company-wide contest to see who could develop a recipe. It was a terrific-tasting drink, but also time-consuming and difficult to make." On the second try, they chose a cocktail that tasted just as good with fewer ingredients.

✓ Name it after your nonprofit organization, or hold a naming contest as a fundraiser. Either way will draw attention to your cause.

✓ Hand out the recipe along with your contact information. For the first fundraiser that featured Roots & Wings' cocktail, Aarini had custom recipe cards created that featured the organization's logo and Web address on the back.

✓ Offer a virgin version, too, so teetotalers won't feel left out of the fun.

✓ Make your cocktail a star! Since its debut, Aarini says, her organization's signature drink has gotten its own Facebook fan page and YouTube videos.

Riya Aarini, Director of Communications, Roots & Wings International, Spokane, WA. Phone (202) 747-4946. E-mail: riya@rootsandwingsintl.org

Pre-Event Supports Nonprofit's Ongoing Efforts

In an effort to support the biggest fundraiser of the year for the Greater Illinois Alzheimer's Association Chapter (Chicago, IL), staff and supporters host a warm-up event. For the past two years, that event has been Purple-tini, a volunteer-hosted fundraiser that benefits the association's programs and services.

An event splashed in purple — the Alzheimer's Association's theme color — Purple-tini offers a fun-loving, relaxed mingling atmosphere for professionals. The ambiance includes specialty martinis, drinks, appetizers and dueling pianos.

Two volunteers spend six months planning details of this pre-event. Tickets are sold at $30 each to the intimate affair that typically attracts 40 to 50 guests on a Saturday evening.

The 2009 event raised $3,500, which will support the organization's largest fundraiser — the Naperville Memory Walk.

Teresa Gruber, manager of special events for the chapter, shares tips from her top volunteer and event organizer, Cathy Rittmueller, for hosting a pre-event fundraiser similar to the Purple-tini:

✓ Work with your network of friends for help. For Purple-tini, the organization brings in the talents of a friend who works in sales at a local printing company and a friend who owns the bar that is used as the venue.

✓ Schedule the event for a time convenient for professionals to attend. Starting too early on a workday eliminates a lot of people who would likely attend otherwise.

✓ Be passionate about the cause. Even small pre-events involve work, and it can get discouraging when people don't respond to your invitation. Be sure not to take that lack of response personally and to always keep the end goal in mind.

Source: Teresa Gruber, Manager-Special Events, Alzheimer's Association-Greater Illinois Chapter, Chicago, IL. Phone (847) 933-2413. E-mail: teresa.gruber@alz.org. Website: www.alzheimers-illinois.org

Light Breakfast Brings in Big Pledges

Girls Inc. of Holyoke (Holyoke, MA) host a simple annual breakfast to raise awareness and secure pledges for its programs that promote the future of girls.

The meal may be light, but the take from the event is hefty, netting more than $125,000 in 2008.

Suzanne Parker, executive director, says the key to the one-hour event's success is to stay on message, stay on schedule and to let the audience hear from the girls the organization serves.

"This event is all about the mission of the organization and we keep it simple," says Parker. "This is a free, one-hour event where people are invited by table captains and at the end, there is an ask."

The event starts promptly at 8 a.m. and ends promptly at 9 a.m., making it a simple way for interested parties to gain information, offer pledges and go on with their day.

The 2008 breakfast featured the theme, "Success: Pass It On," an eight-minute video to give audience members a better feel for the organization's mission and, performances by girls within the organization. The 2009 theme was "Dear World" and the event was held at the Naismith Memorial Basketball Hall of Fame.

The event also offers girls within the organization an opportunity to explore their presentation and leadership skills, says Parker: "We've had Girls Inc. of Holyoke alumni come back and give testimonials, current Girls Inc. members give speeches on how the program has impacted them, and we've had spoken word performances and choruses singing."

With the assistance of more than 70 volunteers — including board members and table captains who work together to bring in 500 guests — Parker says the event brings in people who are ready to pledge.

Costs are kept under $10 a person for yogurt, granola, fresh fruit, coffee, juice and pastries, helping guarantee nearly all funds raised go toward programs and services.

"The whole goal," says Parker, "is to create a broad base of individual supporters within the community."

Source: Suzanne Parker, Executive Director, Girls Inc. of Holyoke, Holyoke, MA. Phone (413) 532-6247.
E-mail: sparker@girlsincholyoke.org

At a Glance —	
Event Type:	Breakfast pledge event
Gross:	$136,000
Costs:	$10,000
Net Income:	$126,000
Volunteers:	71
Planning:	12 months
Attendees:	500
Revenue Source:	Donations by event goers
Unique Feature:	Brief, modest breakfast event

Table Captains Feed Breakfast Success

For the annual breakfast fundraiser for Girls Inc. of Holyoke (Holyoke, MA), table captains invite guests to learn more about and support the organization.

Table captains in the first year consisted of board members who each filled tables of 10, says Suzanne Parker, executive director.

"Assigning table captains has become easier because the event has created so much excitement," Parker says. Currently, the event features 46 table captains who fill tables of 10. She adds that bringing in new faces for more than half the table captain assignments each year helps keep the audience — and event — fresh.

To assign table captains, Parker advises:

❑ The first year of an event, ask board members to act as table captains who then are responsible to invite 10 guests to fill a table at the event.

❑ For future events, ask captains from that year's event to recommend new captains. This oftentimes is a guest from a previous event who is well-connected in the community and has a passion for the organization.

❑ Arm table captains with pledge cards. Invited guests should know up front that they will be attending an ask event where donors are needed. Table captains may also distribute pledge cards to potential guests upon invitation so persons unable to attend can still make a pledge.

Best Ever Directory of Special Events, Fifth Edition.
Edited by Scott C. Stevenson.
© 2010 Stevenson, Inc. Published 2010 by Stevenson, Inc.

Festivals and other community-friendly events appeal to every age. They often represent the celebratory expression of a community's or region's culture. Additionally, they can be quite profitable....

Visually Pleasing Antiques Show Draws Crowds, Raises Funds

For five years, supporters of the Kerr Memorial Museum (Oakmont, PA), a late-1800s house museum, have shaken the dust off the typical antique event to turn it into a major fundraiser.

Kerr Museum's 2009 Antiques Show offered the area's most qualified antique dealers who set up shop at the Oakmont Country Club.

The venue is sectioned off with removable walls to allow dealers to create individual booths, complete with wallpaper, borders and more.

Twenty-four dealers bring in quality antiques that appeal to the collectors throughout the region. All antiques are for sale to the public.

"This is a visually beautiful event," says Joan Stewart, board member of the museum. "It has become our biggest fundraiser."

The event raises funds through event ticket sales, dealer booth fees (based on booth size) and program advertising sales. Organizers invite an exclusive group of guests to attend a preview party the night before the main event. Preview party attendees pay $65 each, which includes hors d'oeuvres and cocktails.

The two-day weekend show is open to the public at a cost of $10 per person.

Although many similar events would also include a silent auction, event organizers of the 2009 show deliberately chose not to follow this course of action.

"We didn't want to take any funds away from the dealers," says Stewart. "We wanted all discretionary income to go to the dealers."

For nonprofits considering hosting an antiques show such as this, Stewart offers three points of advice:

1. **Select a local antiques expert to manage the show.** In the case of the 2009 show, dealers were invited to participate in the event by the show manager who selected only the top, reputable dealers from the region.

2. **If planning your antique show as an annual event, create a logo for the event and use it in all marketing, programs and invitations.** Having this common thread in all pieces creates a look that will catch the eye of attendees as they become familiar with the event. Also, have the event around the same time each year, so you develop a loyal following.

3. **Advertise in publications that appeal to antique collectors.** Kerr Museum's Antique Show organizers advertise heavily in antique magazines and Farm and Dairy magazine — an auction and antiques guide. Don't forget to advertise in local newspapers, magazines and radio.

Source: Joan Stewart, Board Member, Kerr Memorial Museum, Oakmont, PA. Phone: (412) 826-9295.
E-mail: info@kerrmuseum.com

At a Glance —	
Event Type:	Antiques Show
Gross:	$55,000
Costs:	$30,000
Net Income:	$25,000
Volunteers:	50
Planning:	6 months
Attendees:	1,000
Revenue Sources:	Preview party, ticket sales, dealer booth fees, program advertising sales
Unique Feature:	Dealers set up individual "shops" inside local country club

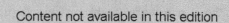

Content not available in this edition

Bargains, Partnerships Drive Boutique Sale Success

A relatively new venture by the Junior League of Baltimore, Inc. (Baltimore, MD) is proving popular with members and the community while raising significant revenue for the nonprofit.

Twice a year, the Junior League hosts a Boutique Warehouse Sale to appeal to its membership of 324 women and to area shoppers. In its first year, the semi-annual boutique sale grossed $60,000. In 2007, the spring sale grossed $75,000 and the fall sale, $50,000. And in 2008, the boutique sale grossed more than $103,000 and netted $55,500 for the organization.

The idea is simple: Ask area boutiques to donate end-of-season or clearance merchandise, then sell the items in a two-day sale, sharing proceeds with the participating boutiques. Any unsold merchandise goes back to the vendor or is added to the Junior League's thrift store.

"We partner with boutiques in the greater Baltimore area, where at the end of the season, they donate merchandise that is unsold," says Laura Pappas, president elect. "They allow us to sell the items at an even greater discount to the public. Some vendors decide to donate all unsold merchandise to the Junior League, after which it becomes inventory in our Wise Penny Thrift Store."

Pappas shares five tips for boutique sales success:

At a Glance —	
Event Type:	Boutique warehouse sale
Gross:	$103,000
Costs:	$47,500
Net Income:	$55,500
Volunteers:	12 to 15 members plus committee chair, co-chair
Planning:	3 months per sale with chair and co-chair working 100-150 hours each
Attendees:	Approx. 550
Revenue Sources:	Sale of clearance and off-season merchandise

1. Survey members to identify connections to locally owned boutiques. In this economy, cold-calling boutique owners can be difficult as they may not be willing to give merchandise unless there is a personal connection with the organization.

2. Ask seasoned members to speak about the mission of the organization and where the boutique sales money will go. Create a talking points sheet for committee members to use when making their presentations.

3. Start on a small, manageable level — partnering with 15 to 20 boutiques — for the first sale, and grow from there.

4. Location, location, location. Location is critical to the success of any boutique event. Pappas says that Baltimore boutique owners felt strongly that the event had to remain in one location so each sale was not a re-education. Also key to the location is whether your organization will have to direct customers to the event through direct marketing or whether it is in a location that already has considerable foot traffic from other stores and restaurants.

5. Ensure that your organization has the resources to pull off the event, which requires many volunteer hours in the days, evenings and weekends leading up to and during the event.

Source: Laura Pappas, President Elect, Junior League of Baltimore, Inc., Baltimore, MD. Phone (410) 435-5521. E-mail: laura@jlbalt.org

Fundraiser Is All in the Family

Staff and supporters of Central Texas Medical Center Hospice Care (San Marcos, TX) have found a way to involve the whole family in its annual fundraiser.

For five years, families have come together to enjoy a Sunday afternoon filled with live music, a silent auction, barbecue buffet and plenty of activities for all ages at the Hats Off for Hospice fundraiser.

"Hospice is a service that is provided for people of all ages," says Lisa Adams, public relations coordinator. "The message is to reach out to families, not certain individuals. Therefore, our mission is to educate and reach out to everyone in the community. We focus on the entire family and their needs."

The family-friendly fundraiser features activities for children, such as a super-sized inflatable Moonwalk, kiddie train and hay wagon rides. Auction items include amusement park tickets, DVD players with family-friendly movies and items autographed by popular child actors.

The 2009 event raised $25,000 with nearly 10 percent of the proceeds coming from youth tickets ($10 for ages 6-17). Adult tickets are $40 for one or $75 for two. Children 5 and younger attend free.

To host a child-friendly fundraiser, Adams says, keep safety in mind.

"Safety is the most important priority," she says. "If you plan to have children attend, make sure that they are safe no matter where they roam.

"The second priority would be entertainment and food. Children need something to keep them busy. If parents are bringing their children to an event, they will also expect that their children will have something to do."

One final tip: Children love treats, so rather than serving dessert with the meal, have a table that sells baked goods — "a great way to generate some extra money."

Source: Lisa Adams, Public Relations Coordinator, Central Texas Medical Center Hospice Care, San Marcos, TX.
Phone (512) 754-6159.
E-mail: lisa.adams@ahss.org

Country Faire Fun for the Whole Family

Dunk tank. Cake walk. Petting zoo. Pony rides. Wii Rock Band station. Train rides.

Everything about the Eureka Schools Foundation's (Granite Bay, CA) Country Faire suggests a focus on the family. That's by design, says Julie Guerrero, executive director.

"Several years ago we surveyed our yearly events and realized our fundraising was directed almost entirely at adults," Guerrero says. "The Country Faire is our way of reaching out to the entire family."

Featuring eight to 10 food booths, 15 to 20 games and activities, and several dozen vendor/information booths, the event regularly draws more than 3,500 participants. With admission free of charge, revenue comes from vendor fees and tickets sold at all activity sites. Participants can purchase all-inclusive wristbands for $40.

Each school recruits students and parents to secure the hundreds of volunteers needed to staff the event. But an online transaction engine provided by greatergiving.com is also key, says Guerrero.

All school websites and the foundation site link to a volunteer page where people can log in and sign up for one- or two-hour blocks of time, she explains. The database-driven software can then produce spreadsheets and reports that are vital to organizing so many volunteers.

The event is unquestionably labor intensive — so much so, the event is held only every other year to prevent volunteer fatigue. Still, it serves an important function, says Guerrero. "It's a feel-good event that showcases everything the foundation does for all the schools we serve."

Held in a public park, the Country Faire involves few out of pocket expenses, and regularly grosses around $35,000.

Source: Julie Guerrero, Executive Director, Eureka Schools Foundation, Granite Bay, CA. Phone (916) 791-4795. E-mail: Julieguerrero@surewest.net

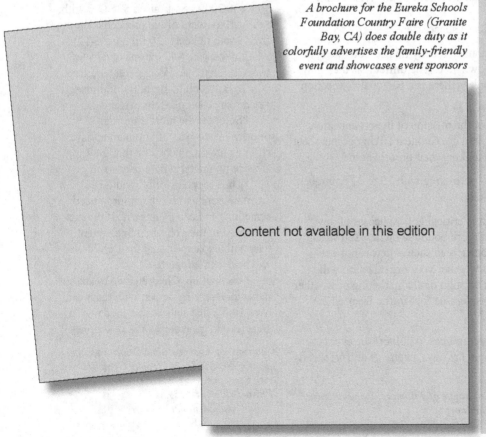

A brochure for the Eureka Schools Foundation Country Faire (Granite Bay, CA) does double duty as it colorfully advertises the family-friendly event and showcases event sponsors

Content not available in this edition

First Annual Event Puts The 'Fun' in Fun Day

The 1st annual Kawasaki Disease Fun Day raised more than $13,000 toward its $25,000 goal before the event even took place.

KD Fun Day was created to support a diagnostic test identifying the disease at the University of California San Diego Disease Research Center (La Jolla, CA). The event, along with supporting donations and sponsors, had raised $26,300, with several events still planned for this summer. Held May 8, 2010, the fun day took place at the Stagecoach Community Park (Carlsbad, CA). Persons paid $10 admission.

Organizers of the fun day share tips to put a similar event in place:

- Create a whimsical flyer that will attract your target audience. See the flyer used by this organization to get a feel for the color, design and content by going to this link: www.kdfunday.org/kd/flyer.cfm.

- Have a popular teen celebrity act as master of ceremonies. During the Kawasaki Disease Fun Day teen celebrity, Jonah Bobo, entertained guests throughout the day.

- Offer family-friendly events such as face painting, balloon animals, music and performances, professional photography, plus drawings and giveaways.

- Find event sponsors that are family- and children-oriented such as rental companies that offer bounce houses, family-friendly restaurants and children's entertainment.

- Choose a wide-open outdoor venue. Stagecoach Community Park offered a vast outdoor location that includes a children's play area and ample restroom facilities.

Source: Nicole Hershman-Daniels, Membership Event Founder & Chair, Kawasaki Disease Fun Day, Oceanside, CA. Phone (760) 433-1469. E-mail: dashnlefty@gmail.com. Website: www.kdfunday.org

Firefly Art Fair Draws Crowds, Funds

For 23 years, the Wauwatosa Historical Society (Wauwatosa, WI) has hosted its Firefly Art Fair, and organizers say the years of experience have paid off. Grossing nearly $35,000 and averaging 5,000 attendees each year, this event has grown to be the historical society's largest fundraiser.

In 2009, more than 90 artists participated in the event by renting outdoor booth space on the historical site's 1.5-acre grounds. Art fair attendees go from booth to booth to view artists' original works, walk through the site's Victorian gardens and visit the historic Kneeland-Walker House. Intermixed throughout the grounds are food vendors who offer homemade pie, sandwiches and beverages, including beer, while live music plays in the background.

The event raises funds from its ticket sales, a silent auction featuring original works donated by participating artists, food and beverage sales and artist booth rental fees.

Janel Ruzicka, the historical society's executive director, offers advice from the seasoned event planners of the 23rd Annual Firefly Art Fair for making similar events successful:

✓ **Consider the economic climate.** After careful consideration, the Firefly Art Fair event planners did not raise their food prices in 2009 even though the cost of the food went up. Additionally, artist fees and ticket pricing remained the same as the previous year to continue to draw a large crowd.

✓ **Ignore the weather.** Ruzicka recommends holding the event rain or shine. When rain falls, she says, attendees actually tend to huddle under vendor tents and tend to buy more items from each vendor in gratitude for the cover.

✓ **Create a pleasant atmosphere for guests.** Offer a variety of options for the guests, from artists booths to historic venue and great food. The Firefly Art Fair prides itself on offering homemade, down-home foods appealing to guests.

✓ **Create a pleasant atmosphere for visiting artists.** Treat artists with the utmost respect. At this art fair, artists are treated to a Saturday evening artist reception and a Sunday morning breakfast.

✓ **Persistence is key.** In the first years of offering an art fair, Ruzicka recommends not building profits into your budget. Also, she says, expect to offer an event such as this for two to three years without gains. Longevity, consistency and building your reputation are the keys to turning an art fair into a significant fundraiser.

Source: Janel Ruzicka, Executive Director, Wauwatosa Historical Society, Kneeland-Walker House & Gardens, Wauwatosa, WI. Phone (414) 774-8672.
E-mail: staff@wauwatosahistoricalsociety.org

At a Glance —

Event Type:	Art Fair
Gross:	$35,000
Costs:	$3,000
Net Income:	$32,000
Volunteers:	100
Planning:	12 months
Attendees:	5,000
Revenue Sources:	Admission fees ($4); food and beverage sales; silent auction; artist booth rental
Unique Features:	Artists pay booth rental to sell art; venue is an historical house open for viewing during art fair

Content not available in this edition

Teddy Bear Hospital Day Reinforces Community Service Efforts

For a fun way to involve the community in the work you do, engage the littlest members first. That's what first-year medical students at Albany Medical Center (Albany, NY) do with Teddy Bear Hospital Day.

Shelby Spandl, medical student and event coordinator, says the event gives children a fun and safe way to get comfortable with the medical field and going to the doctor.

Children from the community are invited to bring a favorite stuffed animal to the hospital. They get a Teddy Bear Hospital Day badge and a passport. They have the passport stamped at stations, including family practice, where they do a physical on their bear with the help of the medical students; the emergency department, where they look at x-rays of teddy bears; and internal medicine, where they play a life-sized Operation game. Bears even visit plastic surgery to have buttons sewn on and rips stitched. The young guests also watch a medical helicopter land and check out an ambulance.

Some 15 youngsters attended the 2009 event, says Standl, noting the day is fun for more than the children. "The students get to apply all they've learned in the clinical skills class," she says. "It's positive publicity for the hospital and a great chance for the community to visit the hospital in a positive situation."

Source: Shelby Spandl, Medical Student and Event Coordinator, Albany Medical College, Albany, NY. Phone (518) 262-5079.
E-mail: spandls@mail.amc.edu

Green Fair Attendees Learn from Experts and By Example

If you're looking to green your event, follow these easy tips from the 2010 Think Green Fair (Rochester, MN), designed to alert attendees to all the innovations in going green.

Average attendance at this event is 3,000 to 5,000 guests who are ecology-minded individuals looking for information from experts on the latest updates in environmentally friendly technology. At this June 2010 event, attendees were educated on:

✓ Earth-friendly home and garden products including eco-friendly household cleaners, composting, rainwater harvesting and more.

✓ Energy efficiency & renewable energy.

✓ Conservation and protection of water and/or air.

✓ Waste reduction.

✓ Durable and reusable products.

✓ Organic or locally produced foods including free-range and pesticide-free.

✓ Green certification: USDA Organic, Energy Star, Fair Trade, LEED.

✓ Health and wellness.

✓ Promotion of environmental values.

To locate experts to appear at this event, Caitlin Meyer, Think Green Fair coordinator, invited environmental experts from the area to host exhibit booths at the fair as well as offer presentations. Additionally, Meyer contacted businesses in the area that specialize in environmentally savvy innovations to showcase their products and services.

Offering a green event means that your event should also recognize awareness in sustainability and green technology. Meyer says the 2010 Think Green Fair incorporated the foll-

Content not available in this edition

owing green philosophies:

✓ A goal of zero waste at the event. Increased recycling and composting opportunities and a conscious effort from vendors and the fair committee to use less paper and non-recyclable materials.

✓ Local and organic food options for fair attendees.

✓ Promote biking and walking!

Source: Caitlin Meyer, Think Green Fair Coordinator, 2010 Think Green Fair, Rochester, MN. Phone (507) 328-6396.
E-mail: meyer.caitlin@co.olmsted.mn.us.
Website: www.neighbors.org/thinkgreen

Pampering Event Promotes Wellness, Local Business

The Henderson Health Care Services Auxiliary (Henderson, NE) offers an event filled with pampering that not only promotes wellness, but local business as well.

Event organizers invite local business owners to participate in helping the community in a wellness effort. Manicurists, cosmetologists, massage therapists and exercise professionals all join in at the event to pamper the community while supporting the programs at Henderson Health Care Services.

In its second year, Spa Night also brought in an athletic clothing expert and an exercise ball instructor. Tickets were $25 in advance or $30 at the door.

Marcia Regier, junior auxiliary president, offers tips to bring together businesses for a successful community wellness event:

✓ Tap into the local businesses since these are the people who use the health care facility (or other nonprofit organization) supported by the event.

✓ Encourage vendors to bring business cards to give to interested event participants, but ask them not to sell their products at the event so you can create a pampering environment, not a sales environment.

✓ Be mindful of health regulations. Organizers of this event opted not to perform pedicures because of the cleanliness issues and inability to sanitize equipment between clients.

✓ Do lots of advertising, including word-of-mouth from members, says Regier, noting: "One of our members brought her niece's wedding party to Spa Night in celebration of her bachelorette party."

Source: Marcia Regier, Junior Auxiliary President, Henderson Health Care Services, Henderson, NE. Phone (402) 723-4512.
E-mail: mmmm@mainstaycomm.net

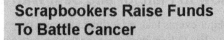
Special Event's Website Encourages Plans and Stories

What began in 1992 as a weekend coat drive in the San Francisco area bringing in 400 coats has grown into One Warm Coat (San Francisco, CA), a nationwide effort that has garnered more than 1 million coats for people in need. This year, representatives anticipate collecting 500,000 coats in 2,500 grassroots coat drives across the nation.

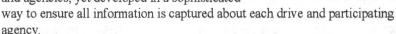

Content not available in this edition

Driving the success of the organization's many events is a website (www.onewarmcoat. org) that is easy to use by drive organizers and agencies, yet developed in a sophisticated way to ensure all information is captured about each drive and participating agency.

"What we have behind the website are two dynamic databases that are really high-tech," says Sherri Lewis Wood, One Warm Coat president and national coordinator. "We present the information in an encouraging way with an unintimidating website."

Coat drive organizers who click on Organize a Drive at the main webpage are directed to five items to help them expedite the drive:

1. **Online Guidebook** — This book walks participants through the steps of hosting a successful coat drive.

2. **Find an Agency** — Those registering for a coat drive find agencies in their area which are in need of coats.

3. **Share Your Plans** — This form registers the coat drive and starts the process for disseminating information electronically to coat drive organizers.

4. **Tools and Resources** — Found here are templates, logos, tax receipts and more for participants use.

5. **Share Your Success** — When a coat drive wraps, the person who registered the drive receives a form to complete outlining the success of the drive. Data about the drive is captured and used by the main office to track numbers.

The website also hosts a Share Your Plan form for planners to register their coat drive. Once registration is complete, planners receive an automated e-mail confirming the entered information. With information confirmed, planners are mailed supplies within two days. Within five days of the drive's conclusion, planners receive another automated e-mail asking for event feedback titled Share Your Success.

The second dynamic database asks agencies in need to complete a Share Your Need form where information collected helps coat drive organizers match their drive with an agency in their region.

Source: Sherri Lewis Wood, President and National Coordinator, One Warm Coat, San Francisco, CA. Phone (877) 663-9276. E-mail: sherri@onewarmcoat.org

Scrapbookers Raise Funds To Battle Cancer

As scrapbooking has become more popular, so too has its use as a fundraising event.

Scrapbook stores, civic groups and community members across the nation host cropping events that can last a few hours, a full weekend or longer to raise money for the Susan G. Komen for the Cure Foundation.

One such event, The Siouxland Crop for the Cure® (Sioux City, IA), has raised more than $21,000 for its local affiliate since 2007. The 12-hour event features scrapbooking, card making, quilting, shopping with on-site vendors, more than 100 auction items, massages, a garage sale of scrapbooking materials, door prizes and snacks.

Jamee Carlson, founder and co-chair, along with a fellow committee member, got the idea to host a scrapbooking event after attending a similar event in a nearby city.

Inspired by her mother-in-law, who is a two-time breast cancer survivor, Carlson got to work immediately recruiting friends to bring her vision to reality.

With no money for publicity, Carlson says she relied on word of mouth, hanging flyers at local businesses and running a newspaper ad in a local paper to reach her audience. A lack of publicity dollars didn't deter attendees, says Carlson, as more than 60 scrappers supported the inaugural event, raising more than $9,500. In 2008, the event drew more than 70 guests and generated more than $11,700.

To make sure 100 percent of the fundraiser's net profits are donated to the local Susan G. Komen affiliate, Carlson says the five-person committee solicits donations and support from local residents and businesses and at times reach into their own pockets to purchase items needed for the event.

Source: Jamee Carlson, Founder and Co-chair, The Siouxland Crop for the Cure®, Hinton, IA. Phone (712) 947-4770. E-mail: sxlandcropforthecure@yahoo.com

How to Plan for and Deal With 25,000 Visitors

Major events take major planning and preparation.

Iris Dillon, director of special events for the Indianapolis Art Center (Indianapolis, IN), organizes the Broad Ripple Art Fair. The fair hosts more than 25,000 visitors in two days, and in 2009 made a net profit of more than $300,000.

After 40 years, part of the art fair's success is its popularity and name recognition. Dillon says that local corporate sponsors eagerly donate money and materials to the fair, because they know it will raise their profile in the community. As such, the art center pays out very little overhead to put on the fair, and can reap more of the profits from the art fair's many elements: $15 ticket sales; concessions; artist fees and applications to participate in the fair; and a student sale (people who have taken classes at the art center have an opportunity to try selling their work without paying a table fee, but they are encouraged to give a portion of their earnings back to the art center).

But securing community support is only half the battle of pulling off the major event each May, Dillon says. "People know and expect the art fair," she says, "but we still have to carry it off." The Art Fair occurs in May, and the To-Do list for Dillon and her 25-person staff begins months before (see box, right).

For organizations considering a major event, Dillon offers the following tips for success:

✓ **Promote staff ownership.** Don't micromanage. If your staff feels connected to their work, they are more likely to succeed.

✓ **Be confident**. Take things as they come — don't create challenges before they arrive. Remember that the second day is harder than the first, and each year is easier than the last!

✓ **Make your message highly visible.** Make sure to connect the fundraiser with the organization you're raising money for.

✓ **Involve the community.** Make sure the neighbors know what's going on, and how they can help. The Broad Ripple Art Fair depends on its 400-plus volunteers every year.

Source: Iris Dillon, Director of Special Events and Broad Ripple Art Fair, Indianapolis Art Center. Indianapolis, IN. Phone (317) 255-2464. E-mail: IDillon@indplsartcenter.org. Website: www.indplsartcenter.org

Event's Unique Advertising Campaign Reaches Out To Large Community

A major event such as the 25,000-attendee Broad Ripple Art Fair requires serious advertising efforts. So Iris Dillon, director of special events at the Indianapolis Art Center (Indianapolis, IN), which hosts the art fair, came up with a creative idea for the event's milestone 40th year.

In addition to advertising in papers, fliers and at sponsor locations, Dillon and her team designed and produced 40 collectible cards to be distributed at various events. These events will take place at the Art Center's sister organizations and restaurants in the Broad Ripple area to raise awareness of the art fair and art center as community members seek to collect all 40 cards and win prizes associated with them.

Planning Key to Hosting Major Event

To orchestrate the Broad Ripple Art Fair, held each May to benefit the Indianapolis Art Center (Indianapolis, IN). Iris Dillon, director of special events, shares the to-do list she prepares for herself and her 25-person staff:

October:
- Review and update contracts with past sponsors.
- Submit for city permits.
- Post artists' call-for-entry in newsletters and online.
- Begin public advertising.
- Schedule committee meetings to begin laying out the timeline.

Committees:

Vendor: Members secure food/drink vendors, later oversee the load-in/load-out of food.

Entertainment: Members secure line-ups for 4 stages, making sure to include diversity in the acts selected.

Marketing: Members raise exposure via posters, postcards, on-site signage, banners, tickets, media sponsorships and contracts.

Artists: Members work with artists to update artist information, address artists' concerns, run the jury process for the art contest.

Student Sale: Members work with artists who have taken classes within a recent time frame; organizes sale of student art.

Facilities/Grounds: Members make sure the grounds are ready for heavy traffic, prepare for rain, ready for trash pick up.

Development: Members are responsible for raising money!

Logistics: Oversees, encourages and helps other committees, while offering hands-on help.

November, ongoing:
- Hold monthly meetings with committee members.
- Secure locations for guest parking.
- Order shuttle buses.
- Secure 25 portable restrooms to supplement indoor restroom facilities. Make sure that a person from the portable restroom service will be on the grounds during the event.
- Secure tables, chairs and tents for presentations in the art center, sponsor displays and art sale.
- Secure golf carts for easy staff/materials transport on grounds.
- Borrow ticket booths, update system by which volunteers will sell and take tickets.

January:
- Begin displaying marketing materials at the Art Center itself.
- Send out any special marketing materials, like 40th anniversary collectible cards.

February:
- Secure food vendors.
- Secure entertainment.
- Secure police support and overnight security.
- Begin thinking about staff assignments for the weekend: covering gates, helping artist, student sale etc.

March-April:
- City-wide marketing push.
- Tickets go on sale.

May: The event happens.

Post event: Follow-up with vendors, sponsors and lots of paying of bills.

Festival Formats: '10 by 10' Offers Bite-size Performances

"10 plays. 10 minutes. 10 performers. 10 bucks."

The motto for "10 by 10 in the Triangle" event for The ArtsCenter (Carrboro, NC) concisely sums up why this short play festival, held each July, has become so popular.

"There are so many reasons why people like this format," says Emily Ranii, artistic director of ArtsCenter stage. "It's exciting because it's different every year. There's also a little bit of something for everyone because we try to reach all ages, men and women —and with 10 plays, you're bound to like at least eight of them."

An art gallery and theater, it has seen attendance grow over the event's eight years, Ranii says, nearly selling out the 325-seat theater on many nights of the festival's two-weekend run. Its success has led Ranii to plan for three weekends for 2010's event.

Planning starts in early January, when Ranii sends out calls for submission of play scripts. She puts the notice on The ArtsCenter's website, sends press releases, e-mails playwrights featured in past festivals and posts it on playwright listservs.

Because of the event's popularity, Ranii says she receives about 400 scripts each year. A group of judges score submissions from 1 to 6 (based on storyline consistency, presence of a conflict and how interesting it is) and pick their three favorites, eventually whittling the list to the 25 finalists.

By the end of May, the year's 10 plays are selected, and the 10 actors have only a month to rehearse their roles. They each handle several roles across all 10 plays.

Ranii notes they try to choose plays that follow a similar theme or idea, creating a more cohesive show series. This July, the plays were linked by a water motif.

Although Ranii says The ArtsCenter pays all of the directors, actors and production team members for their participation each year, there are still tons of volunteers who help make the festival a reality.

Contact: Emily Ranii, artistic director of ArtsCenter stage, The ArtsCenter, Carrboro, NC. Phone (919) 929-2787, ext. 221. E-mail: theatre@artscenterlive.org

Judges Whittle 400 Submissions to 10 Crowd-pleasing Plays

Here is the list of plays featured at the 2009 "10 by 10 in the Triangle" event for The ArtsCenter (Carrboro, NC):

❑ CARJACKED (World Premiere) by Noelle Donfeld with Music by Bonnie Janofsky. A musical. A woman attracts quite a crowd in a parking lot — her four-door Ford has been carjacked! Or is it a shiny red Accord?

❑ FALLINGWATER (World Premiere) by Lauren Yee. She plays Chopin way too loud as water drips from the ceiling. Her ex-boyfriend is taking a three-day bath in the apartment upstairs.

❑ FISSSSHHHH (World Premiere) by Jennifer Maisel. Motherhood as a way of life and as a class project. Goldfish bowls, snow globes and the sweet taste of tears.

❑ GREEN EGGS AND MAMET by Matt Casarino. That guy from Oleanna and a guy from Glenn-garry Glenn Ross at a bar. The profanity of David Mamet written in the rhyme of Dr. Seuss.

❑ LA 8AM (Regional Premiere) by Mark Harvey Levine. A man who reduces everything to numbers — the number of bowls of fruit loops he will eat, the number of times he

will hear "The Pictures of Matchstick Men," the number of fights he will have with his girlfriend. But the question remains: Is love reducible to numbers?

❑ LOVE AND TAXES (World Premiere) By Chuck Keith. A brain, a heart and a surprise.

❑ MELT (World Premiere) by Stephanie Alison Walker. A girl and her grandfather on a glacier. His ear is to the ice and he is melting along with the glacier. Whiteout.

❑ NORMAL IS A COUNTRY by Steven Schutzman. A son is home from Iraq and struggling with language and feelings and the word "I." "Normal is a country where someone strange can live. Strange is an island with a mouth."

❑ ORI & ADDISON (World Premiere) by James C. Ferguson. A father-to-be shows off his homemade crib and stroller. Unwittingly, this proud (albeit thrifty) papa has designed two death traps.

❑ THIS SIDE UP (Regional Premiere) by Lisa Soland. A woman has mailed herself (naked) to a guy. The rule-abiding postal worker refuses to let her out of the box or cut an air hole. Will he turn it right-side-up?

Best Ever Directory of Special Events, Fifth Edition.
Edited by Scott C. Stevenson.
© 2010 Stevenson, Inc. Published 2010 by Stevenson, Inc.

EVENTS THAT INVOLVE COLLEGE-AGED, SCHOOL PARTICIPANTS

Whether they are involved in planning and executing an event or they are participants in it, here are several examples of events that involve or reach out to youth.

College Students Pull All-nighter for Worthy Cause

Students at California State University (Cal State Long Beach), Long Beach, CA, aren't thinking about their grades when they pull an all-nighter for St. Jude Children's Research Hospital (Memphis, TN). Rather, they're thinking about the children being treated at the hospital, as well as their families.

Courtney Day, executive director of Cal State Long Beach's Up 'til Dawn fundraiser, says that since college students pull all-nighters "all the time," it made sense when students at the University of Tennessee created the Up 'til Dawn fundraising event.

"When Cal State and Tri Delta alumni Crystal Blaylock found out about the event, she knew she needed to bring it to our campus since St. Jude is Tri Delta's chosen charity," says Day. "Since its inception at Cal State Long Beach in 2005, the event has raised more than $80,000 for St. Jude," with the 2009 event bringing in an additional $18,000-plus.

Students pay $5 to attend the event, which runs from 6 p.m. until 6 a.m., though they are not required to stay the 12 hours. Attendees are asked to bring names and addresses of family and friends, who are then sent pre-written letters asking for donations to St. Jude.

During the event, those in attendance use the addresses they brought to write out envelopes and are eligible to win prizes based on the number of addresses they bring. Students bringing 75 or more addresses are eligible for a chance to win the grand prize: $2,000 in free tuition.

In addition to sending letters and winning prizes, Day says, students enjoy free food, bands, disc jockeys and other entertainment, as well as giving back and getting involved in the college community. Students can earn community service hours for participating.

The entire event is coordinated by a student-run committee. Approximately 40 volunteers work with Day to count letters, answer questions and act as runners.

Some 450 people attended the 2009 all-night event.

Source: Courtney Day, Executive Director, Up 'til Dawn, California State University at Long Beach, Long Beach, CA.
Phone (562) 243-2069. E-mail: c.day88@yahoo.com

High School Students Shine Light on Event Success

BALTO — Bring A Light to Others. Students at Edmond North High School (Edmond, OK) have been doing that since 1994 through their annual BALTO charity week events.

In 2008, they set a fundraising record at the school and made the single largest gift ever to the Make-A-Wish Foundation of Oklahoma: $179,500.

The program was recognized at the foundation's national conference as the outstanding Kids for Wish Kids® program. Here's how it works:

At the end of each school year, the current BALTO chairs select next year's chairs. Chairs begin meeting with prospective charities in June, and announce their decision in September. They are also responsible for coordinating the planning of the week's events. BALTO candidates are selected from each grade level to energize the student body and lead the fundraising efforts.

A parent meeting is held in October to share information about the recipient organization, BALTO events and what will be expected of the students.

BALTO week is filled with events that raise funds, including a dance marathon, 5K run, pom/cheer clinic, garage sale and carnival.

Students also make donations to receive a wrist band that allows them to attend a variety of assemblies during BALTO week, including the Mr. Husky assembly, where male students compete in pageant-like activities to win over the hearts of the school's secretaries, a.k.a. the judges; and a boy/girl assembly where boys compete against girls in contests and perform dares for donations.

Candidates who raise the most funds in each grade level are named "Prince" and "Princess," with "King" and "Queen" titles going to students who raise the most funds overall.

Organizers are again setting their sights high for the 2009 event, which they hope will raise a record $134,000.

Source: Kandy Parsons, Director of Donor Relations, Make-A-Wish Foundation of Oklahoma, Oklahoma City, OK.
Phone (405) 286-4000. E-mail: kparsons@oklahoma.wish.org

> #### Common Thread Unites Efforts
>
> Students at Edmond North High School (Edmond, OK) have had great success raising funds for the local community through their BALTO charity week events.
>
> The community's two other local high schools also hold charity events to raise funds for causes of their choosing.
>
> Before giving money to their chosen organizations, students from the three schools work together to identify a "common thread" — an organization that all three schools agree to support — and each donates 5 percent of their respective event's proceeds to that organization.

Event Inspires Students, Promotes Literacy, Raises Funds

It began in 1996 with a simple question: What would it be like to get an author like science fiction legend Ray Bradbury to come to Ogden, UT?

That year, Ray Bradbury did come to the Utah town of 80,000, and the Ogden School Foundation has been attracting world-class talent to its annual Fall Author Event ever since.

The event provides educational enhancement to district students, says Janis Vause, the foundation's executive director, but it is an important fundraiser as well. It sells out its 900-seat venue months in advance, and though author fees range from $5,000 to $40,000, the author dinner regularly nets $55,000 to $65,000.

The event begins with an afternoon social hour and book sale. At dinner, a short DVD highlights foundation projects, and organizers reveal the identity of next year's author. The centerpiece is the author presentation and book signing, a combination that can last hours.

For organizations interested in hosting a similar event, she recommends looking for an inside person to help.

"An English professor, library or bookstore employee, even a donor who attends writing conferences and might have made informal contacts — any kind of personal connection will help distinguish you from the crowd," she says.

Alternatively, she says, approach author agents directly. Contact information can be found on authors' websites, and handling such requests is part of an agent's job.

Source: Janis B. Vause, Executive Director, Ogden School Foundation, Ogden, UT. Phone (801) 737-7307. E-mail: vausej@ogdensd.org

At a Glance —	
Event Type:	Author Dinner
Gross:	$100,000
Costs:	$40,000
Net Income:	$60,000
Volunteers:	45
Participants:	900
Planning:	14 months
Revenue Sources:	Ticket sales, private sponsorship
Unique Feature:	Consistently top-flight authors

Students Dance Their Way Into Community's Heart

The right mix of entertainment and opportunity to help a worthy cause can sometimes create an event that spans generations.

The South High Dance Marathon (SHMD), South Glens Falls, NY, has raised $2.8 million in 32 years to benefit individuals and organizations in the community, including the Juvenile Diabetes Research Foundation and the Ronald McDonald House.

The event that started with about 50 dancers raising some $1,500 for the local rescue squad has grown to include more than 600 dancers raising $260,000 in 2009.

Students from South Glens Falls High School organize the dance and select fund recipients. The dance begins on Friday evening and continues, with activities and breaks interspersed, until 10 p.m. Saturday. The 28-hour event concludes with a grand finale featuring awards for students raising the most money, raffle drawings, the live auction and the announcement of the total amount raised.

Last but not least, the dancers present a Strut Your Stuff performance, says Megh Howard, who manages the event's website.

Howard says attendees enjoy great entertainment plus a multitude of opportunities to make donations at the event, including purchase of raffle tickets, 50/50 tickets and SHMD apparel. Attendees also contribute through vendors who sell snacks and cut hair for donations, and the live and silent auctions. Says Howard, "Every year SHMD depends greatly on the kind hearts and undying generosity of the South Glens Falls community ... and they never disappoint!"

Source: Megh Howard, Website Manager, South High Dance Marathon, South Glens Falls, NY. Phone (518) 824-1229. E-mail: megh247@hotmail.com

College Partners Spice Up Successful Annual Event

For many attendees, the High Noon Chili Shoot-Out of the Ronald McDonald House Charities (RMHC) of Phoenix, AZ is simply a tasty way to support a worthy cause.

Area schools Collins College (Tempe, AZ), Sanford-Brown College (Phoenix, AZ) and Le Cordon Bleu College of Culinary Arts (Scottsdale, AZ) had all expressed interest in partnering with the RMHC, says Leslie Tan, RMHC development manager. "All it took was a representative from one of the colleges pitching the idea to us and the other two schools for the cook-off to get started."

With support from all quarters, a seven-member planning committee was quickly formed. Meeting weekly, the group that included Tan and representatives from the colleges set out to tackle logistics by specialty area. The culinary school handed all food-related matters. The graphic arts college directed design work and signage. The RMHC built and administered an event website.

The strengths of individual committee members were utilized as well. One detail-minded registrar managed coordination of volunteers and day-of logistics. Another member, a director of education, used connections to secure judges for the contest.

For organizations eyeing a collaborative event, Tan suggests focusing on each partner's strengths and resources. "Having people doing things in their realm of expertise which they can get excited about makes everything, including collaboration, run a lot smoother," she says.

Source: Leslie Tan, Development Manager, Ronald McDonald House Charities of Phoenix, AZ, Phoenix, AZ. Phone (602) 264-5670. E-mail: Ltan@rmhcphoenix.com

Student-driven Event Raises $1 Million Over Five Years

Since 2004, National Honor Society high school students from Northport High (Northport, NY) have planned and organized A Midwinter Night's Dream — a special event that raises funds for Amyotrophic Lateral Sclerosis (ALS) research.

Students established the event five years ago after teacher David Deutsch was diagnosed with ALS, also known as Lou Gehrig's Disease. They initially organized a three-on-three basketball tournament and raised $32,000 for ALS research. After attending a major ALS fundraiser in New York City, the students decided they wanted to do more.

The first annual event, A Midwinter Night's Dream, raised $90,000.

The 2009 event drew 550 guests to Oheka Castle on Long Island and raised $345,000, bringing the five-year fundraising total to $1,067,000. In addition, in June 2009 they opened their own research lab, entitled A Midwinter Night's Dream Cryopreservation Lab, at Stony Brook University Medical Center (Stony Brook, NY).

Throughout the year, the students contact companies to ask for sponsorships to the event. Sponsor names appear in a commemorative journal given to all event guests.

Event tickets are $150 per person and raffle tickets (winner gets to choose one of three vacations) generate significant funds. The gala features live entertainment, dinner, a student-run presentation and silent and live auctions.

"Our organization is motivated completely by the local ALS patients we visit each month," says Don Strasser, executive director of A Midwinter Night's Dream. "It's important that the students see who we are fighting for.... It not only inspires the students to continue to fight against ALS, but also gives hope to the patients and their families. In addition to this, we send students to prestigious research centers over the summer to observe and conduct ALS research. This gives the students the opportunity to see where the money we raise goes and how much the research facilities need it."

Source: Don Strasser, Executive Director, A Midwinter Night's Dream, Northport High School National Honor Society, Northport, NY. Phone (631) 262-7428. E-mail: dstrasser9@optonline.net. Website: www.amnd.org

---

Tips to Maximize Student-driven Success

For five years, Don Strasser has successfully managed students at Northport High School National Honor Society (Northport, NY) as they raised funds for ALS research through the popular event, a Midwinter Night's Dream. Strasser shares tips for managing a young group of event organizers:

- **Treat it like a job.** "Students are chosen for our organization based on an application and interview process, much like applying for a job. This narrows a large group of students down to a smaller, more motivated group of about 40 willing to do extra work to get things done. It also teaches students to work hard for something they want instead of just handing it to them (and) proves to the advisors that these students will make a positive impact on the organization because they have the will to work more than others."

- **Connect them to the cause.** "Students work so much better if they have a reason to. Teach them about the cause, introduce them to inspirational people and get them excited about what they have ahead. If there is no connection to the cause, the fundraising will be harder and not as successful."

- **Encourage communication.** "We e-mail each other constantly about tasks that need to be completed, important events, good news, etc. Without good communication and monthly meetings, we are unable to work together as a successful team."

- **Give them individual goals.** "Each year, we give the students personal goals that they are encouraged to complete by the event. For example, each committee member is asked to raise $5,000 for A Midwinter Night's Dream as a personal fundraising goal. They are also asked to sell a certain amount of raffle tickets.... They motivate each other to get their jobs done."

- **Keep them in the loop.** "If you keep them updated on important developments and news within the organization, they become more motivated and excited about their jobs. For example, we keep the students updated about how much money we have raised so far this year so they know what needs to be done to complete the year's goal."

Best Ever Directory of Special Events, Fifth Edition.
Edited by Scott C. Stevenson.
© 2010 Stevenson, Inc. Published 2010 by Stevenson, Inc.

Themes can significantly impact an event's success. If carried out creatively and to the last detail, themes provide a wow factor that will keep guests talking for weeks following your event. Be sure to include some creative types on your committee when selecting and planning every detail of an event theme.

March Martini Madness Mixes Sophistication, 1960s Style

The style! The sophistication! The cocktails!

Why did the Yakima Valley Museum (Yakima, WA) turn to AMC's hit show "Mad Men" for a new fundraising theme?

Demographics, says David Lynx, associate director.

"We had a solid base of patrons, but we were looking for ways to reach out to that 25-to-55 age range," Lynx says. "The mad atmosphere of March Martini Madness created a cool, hip kind of ambiance that really spoke to the crowd we were targeting."

The nighttime event in the museum's neon garden atrium oozed retro 1960s elegance at every turn with gourmet hors d'oeuvres, cigarette girls selling raffle tickets and rat pack music sung by a wandering crooner.

Also central to the event's appeal were three individually themed martini bars. Staffed by bartenders dressed like Marilyn Monroe, Frank Sinatra and James Bond, each sold two or three specialized martinis. A juice bar provided stylish concoctions to those avoiding alcohol.

The sold-out event raised more than $12,000. More importantly, organizers say, it drew a new and younger group of supporters. Lynx estimates that half of the 200 guests were first-time supporters, and he expects that number to grow for future events through strong word-of-mouth promotion.

"People were telling everyone how great a time they had, and there is a lot of excitement for the second Martini Madness," he says, adding that museum staff are already pursuing more robust corporate underwriting to help translate community interest into usable revenue.

Source: David Lynx, Associate Director, Yakima Valley Museum, Yakima, WA. Phone (509) 248-0747. E-mail: David@ yakimavalleymuseum.org

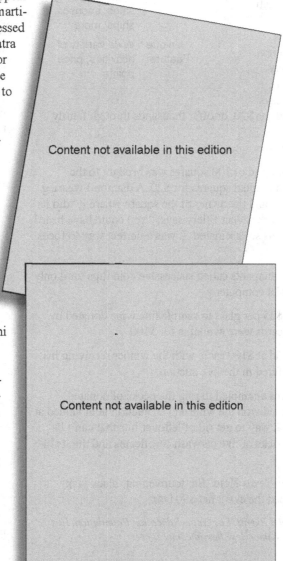

Content not available in this edition

Content not available in this edition

Host a Summer Beach Party to Engage Young

To engage potential donors at a young age and celebrate summer, officials at Salve Regina University (Newport, RI) hosted The Bash at the Beach, a seaside party in a historical and touristy part of town.

"We knew younger alumni would be around town during the summer, but wouldn't be coming to campus. So we decided to take the fundraising party to them," says Brian Kish, assistant vice president for advancement at Salve Regina University and annual giving consultant with Campbell & Company (Chicago, IL).

Kish shares summer bash secrets:

❑ Hold the event at a well-loved bar or restaurant with a deck or on the water.

❑ Charge a ticket price that serves as the donor's contribution and earns the donor two drinks, food, parking and a gift. Build the fair market value of those items into the ticket price, with enough left over to earn a healthy percentage for your organization.

❑ Aim your marketing techniques at younger donors — advertise in recent alumni publications, organizations for young professionals and online.

Source: Brian Kish, Assistant Vice President for Advancement, Salve Regina University, Newport, RI, and Annual Giving Consultant, Campbell & Company, Chicago, IL. Phone (401) 847-6650. E-mail: annualGiving@campbellcompany. com or brian.kish@salve.edu

Branding, Varied Activities Ensure a Dazzling Event

The annual fundraiser of the Los Gatos Education Foundation (Los Gatos, CA) needed tweaking. While the event was raising money, the confusion attendees seemed to have about proper attire suggested problems with branding and messaging, says Kimberley Ellery, director of special events.

The solution? Denim and Diamonds.

"The theme really established the tone of the evening," Ellery says. "The décor was casual but elegant — red roses and crystal — and the guests looked fabulous. They were very comfortable in their jeans, but outstanding in their jewelry."

Organizers wove the diamond motif throughout the event, from promotional artwork to a jeweler selling diamonds (and donating a portion of the proceeds to the foundation) at the event itself.

While the theme got people in the door, Ellery credits the variety of activities for securing their support. "We were very deliberate about offering many levels of participation at different price points," says Ellery. "People could jump in for as little as $20, or offer thousands through family sponsorships."

The event's many activities included:

At a Glance —	
Event Type:	Themed Gala
Gross:	$135,000
Costs:	$45,000
Net Income:	$90,000
Volunteers:	6
Planning:	9 to 12 months
Attendees:	275
Revenue Sources:	Ticket sales, live and silent auctions, blackjack tables, poker tourney, jewelry sales, sponsorships, more
Unique Feature:	Wide variety of activities, price points

- **Chicken Bingo.** A fenced, 7X7-foot grid of 100 squares was brought to the dance floor and attendees bought individual squares for $20. A diamond-wearing chicken was then placed on the grid, and the owner of the square where it "did its business" won diamond earrings. Of the event Ellery says, "You could have heard a pin drop in that room, everyone was so fascinated. It was a perfect way to focus attention for the auction."

- **Heads or Tails Raffle.** For $30, participants called successive coin flips until only one remained, winning an iPad tablet computer.

- **Premium Wine Bar.** Guests paid $25 per glass to sample fine wine donated by local vineyards. Five-glass punch cards were available for $100.

- **Best of Raffle.** 100 tickets were sold at $100 each, with the winner receiving his or her choice of any single item offered in the live auction.

- **Wine Toss.** For $15 a toss, attendees attempted to ring the necks of donated bottles of wine. Those who succeeded won the wine and an auction item valued at $50 or less. Ellery says, "It's a great way to get rid of leftover bits that can't be easily packaged or auctioned off, packs of five carwash certificates and things like that."

Other activities including a ticketed Texas Hold 'Em tournament, black jack tables, and live and silent auctions helped the event net $90,000.

Source: Kimberley Ellery, Director of Special Events, Los Gatos Education Foundation, Los Gatos, CA. Phone (408) 402-5014. E-mail: KimberleyEllery@comcast.net

Volunteer Support Adds Enchantment to Event

Special volunteers helped make the Princess Party for the Children & Families of Iowa (CFI) of Des Moines, IA, a special event that enchanted attendees while raising money for the nonprofit.

The October 2009 Princess Party event drew more than 600 attendees for a day of princess-like pampering. Nearly 50 volunteers offered assistance with activities including meeting real princesses, getting autographs, creating princess crafts, having glamour makeovers, enjoying breakfast and games, and watching a special screening of the princess-themed movie, "Enchanted," at a local theater.

Susan Joynt, CFI events manager, shares techniques to recruit appropriate volunteers for a similar event:

❑ Call on a local university sorority to get volunteers willing to dress as princesses and ask them to volunteer in the craft area of your event.

❑ Ask a local birthday party business to provide princess volunteers and costumes that will enchant guests.

❑ Don't forget to ask real royalty to volunteer. At the CFI event, Miss Iowa and Miss Teen Iowa were asked to attend, adding to the royal theme.

Source: Susan Joynt, Events Manager, Children & Families of Iowa, Des Moines, IA.
Phone (515) 697-7961.
E-mail: susanj@CFIOWA.org.
Website: www.givetocfi.org

Dance-themed Gala Raises Funds, Awareness

A unique name and a memorable theme combine in an annual gala that raises money for Children & Families of Iowa (CFI) of Des Moines, IA.

The 2009 Tango raised more than $177,000 and drew 467 attendees — with each $86 ticket sold representing one night of shelter and services for one victim.

"The name for the event used to be Tango on the Terrace because we had it outside on a terrace overlooking the city," says Susan Joynt, event manager. "However, we ran into bad weather, either rain or very high temperatures, year after year that caused us to move the event inside, so we shortened the name to Tango. We use different dance names for levels of giving, Tango being the highest level of corporate support, then Salsa, Rumba and Mamba."

With the additional funds raised through sponsorships and auctions, event organizers estimate the proceeds from the 2009 event will provide 2,000 nights of shelter and services at CFI's domestic violence programs or a month of care for a capacity shelter.

The nonprofit provides shelter, advocacy and outreach for more than 7,000 victims of domestic violence every year. CFI reports that in the past year, the program has seen a 38 percent increase in crisis calls and 13 percent increase in need for safe shelter.

In the past five years, the organization has served more than 44,000 persons.

Follow these tips offered by event planners at CFI to produce a quality gala event:

❑ Establish a good reputation. CFI is an established nonprofit with a good reputation in the community. The Tango gala event is also well-established in its seventh year.

❑ Establish the cause for guests. The money raised is designated to support CFI's domestic violence services.

❑ Tie the event in to the cause. Tango ticket pricing directly reflects the cost of one night of shelter and services for a person fleeing a violent situation.

Source: Susan Joynt, Events Manager, Children & Families of Iowa, Des Moines, IA.
Phone (515) 697-7961. E-mail: susanj@CFIOWA.org. Website: www.givetocfi.org

At a Glance —

Event Type:	Gala event
Gross:	$177,000-plus
Costs:	$31,000
Net Income:	$147,000
Volunteers:	20 to 25 (to solicit corporate donations and silent auction donations; help with catering, invitations and set up)
Planning:	6 to 8 months
Attendees:	467
Revenue Sources:	Ticket sales, corporate sponsorship, live and silent auctions
Unique Feature:	Ticket price based on cost to provide one night of service in domestic violence shelter

Content not available in this edition

Tune Into a TV-themed Event

What do you get when you mix the Dixieland stars-and-bars of "Dukes of Hazzard," elegant candelabras of "Dynasty," and khaki fatigues of "M*A*S*H"?

If you're the Rotary Club of Pottsville (Pottsville, PA), you get TV Night in Pottsville, the theme of its second annual Necho Allen Night fundraiser dinner. The 2010 event drew 200 participants and raised $2,800 for four local charities.

Mary Sitcoske, club secretary, says guests pay $25 for a night of TV-themed fun featuring complimentary beverages, music from a professional DJ and a small Chinese auction.

But the evening's top features are the costumes and table decorations. TV dramas, sitcoms, commercials and sports teams all have their supporters, and competition is stiff for awards such as best costume, most original idea and most creative presentation of theme.

For people uncomfortable with the idea of dressing as favorite TV characters, Sitcoske simply shares photos of past events. "When people see what others have done, their imagination immediately takes off," she says. "Once they have a few ideas of their own, they get excited and start thinking about inviting friends and acquaintances."

Source: Mary Sitcoske, Secretary, Rotary Club of Pottsville, Pottsville, PA.
Phone (570) 628-2969.
E-mail: Msitcoske@verizon.net

Black Tie Optional, Hiking Boots Mandatory for Hiker's Ball

When planning your next event, get creative to host a special event that celebrates your organization's mission while providing a fresh, fun opportunity for attendees.

Adirondack Mountain Club's (Lake George, NY) director of membership & development, Deborah Zack, had an idea buzzing around in her head for years — a formal affair celebrating persons who are active hikers and paddlers, but who also enjoy dancing and the opportunity to socialize.

The idea became a reality in 2009 at the club's first Black Fly Affair: A Hiker's Ball, which raised more than $43,500 for the organization.

What made the event such a success the first time out? One factor that Zack says people really picked up on was the unique dress theme, Black Tie Optional — Hiking Boots Mandatory.

The 350 guests took the theme and ran with it, she says. "Some came dressed in tuxes and formal gowns, some in cocktail dresses and some in kilts. One man even came in khakis with a piece of black tape covering his fly. But every one of them was in hiking boots!"

To boost interest and carry on the creative theme, Zack says, they carried the concept through on the marketing materials as well. Zack and her designer added hiking boots to an image of dancing silhouettes. They also used boot prints and dance steps in the invitations mailed to 5,000 members and donors.

To garner further attention, Zack and her team marketed it using their member magazine, which reaches 20,000 households, on the organization's website, and in newspaper print ads, online calendars, local public radio spots and flyers. They also sent press releases to regional media outlets.

Another selling point was the event location — in the Adirondack mountains at a site overlooking beautiful Lake George. Guests enjoyed a wine tasting from a local winery and ale tastings from a local brew master, along with a chocolate fondue fountain and several food stations. The evening was rounded out with silent and live auctions, and dancing to favorites from the 1940s, '50s, '60s and '70s, including fox trots, Lindys, cha-chas, swing and rock and roll.

To generate excitement for the second annual event, held May 21, 2010, organizers featured online registration on the front page of the organization's website (www.adk.org) that showed the silhouette images of the hiking boot-wearing dancing couple and the phrase, "Be part of the buzz — no, *be* the buzz!" Attendees paid $45 a ticket with the option of making an additional tax-deductible contribution to benefit the nonprofit club.

Source: Deborah Zack, Director, Membership & Development, Adirondack Mountain Club, Lake George, NY . Phone (518) 668-4447. E-mail: deb@adk.org. Website: www.adk.org

What Happens After Event is Key to Its Ongoing Success

It's no secret that events are immensely labor-intensive. That's why Deborah Zack, director, membership & development, Adirondack Mountain Club (Lake George, NY) says the most important part of any event is what happens after it's over:

"Having a good cultivation plan is key. Think about what you want to get out of the event. People have many ways of supporting your organization. Ask how the event-goers wish to get more involved and think about how you can get them more involved."

Content not available in this edition

Content not available in this edition

Fundraiser Celebrates Arts, Culture, Local Heritage

Take your guests on a trip to the past with a night that celebrates the best a prior time had to offer.

The Ozark Arts Council (Harrison, AR) successfully created a first-time fundraiser that celebrated the arts, culture and local heritage.

"'One Night in '29' was designed as an interactive celebration of the arts, and it was our annual fundraiser," says Rachael Prevatte, executive director. "This event encouraged guests to relive the 1920s through the arts in the newly renovated buildings.

"The event featured live music, theater, dance and film and was set in two historic treasures — the 1929 Lyric Theater and the 1929 Hotel Seville."

Guests received a welcome similar to that of the Academy Awards — a lit marquee, the red carpet and interviews with local TV station celebrities, with the images of the arrivals projected on the Lyric's big screen via live feed.

"The red carpet provided a chance to make a grand entrance," Prevatte says. "Most people took the time to learn about the dress style, with some even arriving in vintage clothing. The red carpet allowed everyone to see what everyone else was wearing. It also made the evening feel special. It was a great marriage of technology and nostalgia."

When grand entrances were complete, guests screened a clip from the first film that played in the Lyric and enjoyed brief dance and jazz performances. Actors from the theater company, in character as gangsters, also welcomed everyone to the event.

Guests then moved to the Hotel Seville where the evening continued with additional performances, dinner and a live and silent auction.

The arts council executive director offers inspiration for organizations looking to create a themed event: "Use what you have to create a unique event. Look around for what makes your area/organization unique and build on that.

"Also, keep your mission in mind," she says. "Our mission is to promote the arts. At the planning table we didn't just talk about how much money we could generate with the event, we considered our mission of promoting the arts as a valuable product. This event made some money, but it also reached some who had never attended an event in the Lyric before. It was new, exciting and different."

Source: Rachael Prevatte, Executive Director, Ozark Arts Council and 1929 Lyric Theater, Harrison, AR. Phone (870) 391-3504. E-mail: ozarkartscouncil@gmail.com

"(Live video feed of people arriving on the red carpet) was a great marriage of technology and nostalgia."

At a Glance —	
Event Type:	Interactive fundraiser and arts celebration
Gross:	$15,300
Costs:	$5,000
Net Income:	$10,300
Volunteers:	12
Planning:	5 months
Attendees:	160
Revenue Sources:	Ticket sales, live and silent auctions, event donations and general donations
Unique Feature:	1920s theme that celebrates local heritage

Hair-raising Event Draws Crowd

Tap people's nostalgia for simpler times with a fun event that celebrates smile-inducing aspects of days gone by.

Need an example? Check out the big-hair, mall-bangs-and-mousse era of the 1970s and '80s that is alive and well at the Big Hair Ball at Des Moines Art Center (Des Moines, IA). Begun in 2004, the annual event raises awareness of art center amenities.

At the ball, coiffure and couture meet to create an eye-catching night of fashion and art. The evening is treated as a runway show where local salons create the tallest and most creative coifs to entertain and amuse guests. For the 2009 event, salons were required to complete an entry form before being invited to participate.

Salon personnel work closely with designers to create living art with extravagant hair and trendsetting fashion, says Lauren Rusco, membership manager.

Drawing 800 attendees, the event is particularly well-attended by young fashionistas and the Art Noir group who are the art center's up-and-coming members, Rusco says.

Not only do professional stylists create impressive updos for models, the art center also offers styling, body art, manicurists and makeup artists who tend to guests.

"Attendees come in the most original and imaginative costumes I have ever seen at an event," says Rusco. "You don't have to worry about being the only person with big hair."

While the event raises a modest $2,000 to $3,000, she says gains the art center receives from the event's notoriety and publicity are immeasurable. A local entertainment magazine posts a cover story, while art center personnel use the online social networking sites Twitter and Facebook as well as e-mail lists to create excitement for the event.

"This is a community-building event in celebration of diversity and creativity," says Rusco. She adds that it takes about 10 months for a 10-member committee to plan. Some 100 volunteers help out the day of the ball.

Source: Lauren Rusco, Membership Manager, Des Moines Art Center, Des Moines, IA. Phone (515) 277-4405. E-mail: lrusco@desmoinesartcenter.org

Theatre Guild Brings Experience of Tony Awards to Life

Staff and supporters with the Theatre Guild at Proctors (Schenectady, NY) were looking for a way to raise funds with an exciting event that was the outgrowth of the love they had for Broadway Theater.

The result? Tony Night, a popular event since 2006.

With the opening of the expanded theater in 2007, guests now enjoy the unique experience of viewing the CBS Broadcast of the Tony Awards on a giant Iwerks movie screen, located inside of Proctors' own GE Theatre. The GE Theatre has retractable stadium seating that gives the planners the option of having attendees sit at tables instead of the usual theatre seating. As a result, guests are able to enjoy a fabulous, four-course dinner served at their table during the broadcast.

Judy Decker, events manager, says this popular special event really is all about guests experiencing the feeling of being celebrities for the special night. To that end, guests arrive on the red carpet, which leads to a champagne reception held in the atrium lobby outside of the theatre. Throughout the evening, guests are treated to live entertainment during the broadcast's commercial breaks and witness the honoring of local talent through the Proctors Regional Arts Awards.

Decker says guests are also able to participate in a "theatergoer's dream of a silent auction with performance tickets, artwork and celebrity items up for grabs." For example, auction bidders had the opportunity to bid on tickets to the American Theatre Wing's Tony Awards 2010 at Radio City Music Hall.

To add to the evening's fun, guests are given ballots, and can follow along, voting for their favorite Broadway performers.

In the end though, Decker says the most unique feature of the evening remains the venue. "Guests comment to us that seeing the Tony's on the huge screen makes them feel like they are among the celebrities. Making an event successful is really about bringing a unique event or experience to life for people."

The 120 people who attended Tony Night 2009 raised more than $14,000 through ticket sales, sponsorships and the silent auction.

Source: Judy Decker, Events Manager, Proctors, Schenectady, NY. Phone (518) 382-3884. E-mail: jdecker@proctors.org

Organization's Theme Ties Into Event — Supporting Literacy

Each year, Literacy Instruction for Texas (LIFT) of Dallas, TX, works to engage and support nearly 8,500 adult learners in their quest for literacy. For 48 years, LIFT has been enhancing lives through literacy by orchestrating 157 classes at 15 sites taught by more than 500 volunteers each week.

To celebrate and support the organization's efforts, the organization hosts an annual Champions of Literacy Luncheon, which draws some 300 people a year.

Tahra Taylor, interim executive director, answers questions about the event:

How are funds raised at the event? How much was raised at the most recent event?

"Prior to the event, we raised funds through table sponsorships and individual ticket sales. At the event, we raised funds by selling individual tickets at the door, raffle tickets for prizes, and autographed copies of the speaker's books. Our last event raised approximately $48,000 after expenses."

In what ways do you honor literacy at the event?

"At the September 2009 event, world-renowned mystery author Deborah Crombie was the keynote speaker and she generously agreed to allow LIFT to include the naming of a character in her next book as a raffle prize. Other ways that we tie in literacy to the event is to hold the event in September during National Literacy month and select a theme tied to literacy. Our theme last year was LIFT Off With Books, and the luncheon was held at the Frontiers of Flight Museum in Dallas. We also select one of our adult learners to read his or her story and show a video about LIFT to demonstrate the impact of our programs in the lives of our students and future generations. Last year we used decorated stacks of books as centerpieces and the centerpiece was given to a guest at each table."

At the 2008 event, you were looking for signed books from authors of all genres — how did you use those books?

"In 2008 we received over 300 books. This year we received three book titles without sending a formal request. These books were included in baskets we assembled for raffle items."

What is your best tip for locating authors and getting them to donate signed copies to a fundraising event?

"My best tip is to send the author a request for donated signed copies of his or her book(s). I also suggest asking board members, volunteers and donors if they are aware of authors who might donate one or more of their books for the event."

Source: Tahra Taylor, Interim Executive Director, Literacy Instruction for Texas, Dallas, TX. Phone (214) 824-2000. E-mail: ttaylor@lift-texas.org. Website: www.lift-texas.org

Fundraising in a Soft Economy: Gamble and Gain Big

With the economy in a slump, staff and supporters of Aid for AIDS of Nevada (AFAN), Las Vegas, NV, knew they would have to take drastic steps to make the organization's popular — but highly unconventional — Black & White Party a success.

By making three significant changes, they found out that not playing it safe could pay off big. How big? AFAN saw a 57 percent jump in attendance and $40,000 boost in revenue for the 2009 event compared to 2008, just by making a few simple changes.

Popular Event Grows From Simple Barbecue to Sophisticated Soiree

The Black & White Party started 23 years ago as a backyard, poolside birthday party for two men who requested that, in lieu of gifts, invitees bring canned goods to donate to AFAN. As the guest list has grown, the party has moved to bigger and better locations, morphing from a simple barbecue to a decadent sampling of foods from 13 of the finest restaurants in the city and spirits from nine vendors.

However, attire remains the same: black and white.

"The black-and-white attire and theme really came from the barcodes on the (donated food) cans," says Jennifer Morss, AFAN executive director. "Of course, now with 2,800 people attending the party, we've had to discontinue accepting canned goods, because it's just too much to deal with, but we've always kept the theme the same."

Fresh Venue, Cheaper Tickets, Social Networking Boost Bottom Line

So what helped make the 2009 event such an overwhelming success? A fresh venue, lower ticket prices and using social networking to spread the word.

"We knew that with the economy what it was and with this being a more unconventional fundraiser, we had to do something to generate a higher attendance," Morss says. "It's a party, not a family event, and that already makes it harder to secure corporate sponsorships. We started by lowering ticket prices because it's much easier to spend $35 than it is to spend $50 right now. We also knew that we needed to

Content not available in this edition

come up with a different venue. We'd been at our old venue for five years and it was time to move on."

With a generous donation of space, security, staff and product from the Hard Rock Café Las Vegas (in exchange for a promise from AFAN to sell a block of rooms at a discounted rate) and with the lowered ticket prices, sales skyrocketed.

While Morss and her colleagues were pleased, she says they were also a bit surprised: "We didn't expect this kind of turnout.... We had hoped to raise at least $80,000, but to hit $120,000 was just amazing. As a bonus, we sold out the Hard Rock — even their new tower that they just opened."

Shift From Printed to Electronic Advertising Methods Kicks Up Attendance

Morss and staff did the majority of their marketing via social media. All ticket sales were done online and billboards were digital as well. They used social media sites like Facebook and Twitter to promote ticket sales and offer additional discounts to fans.

"We promised a lot of marketing for in-kind donations as well," Morss adds. "We have a database of 30,000 people, so we promised a lot of exposure for any companies willing to donate funds or materials. And with e-blasts going out every other week in the months before the event, and then every week the month of the event, we feel that we lived up to our promise."

Source: Jennifer Morss, Executive Director, Aid for AIDS of Nevada, Las Vegas, NV. Phone (702)382-2326. E-mail: Jennifer@afanlv.org

Best Ever Directory of Special Events, Fifth Edition.
Edited by Scott C. Stevenson.
© 2010 Stevenson, Inc. Published 2010 by Stevenson, Inc.

Auctions (both silent and live), and raffles add fun and profit to any special event. Although what's being auctioned or raffled matters, the manner in which items are showcased equally impacts their success.

Firefighters Give Their All for Charity Auction

A live auction is at the heart of the annual fundraiser for the Idaho Federation of Families for Children's Mental Health (Boise, ID).

But this isn't your typical auction.

Up for bid? Fifteen tuxedo-wearing bachelors.

And these weren't your typical bachelors.

The well-dressed gentlemen up for bid included firefighters from area departments, smoke jumpers and members of hotshot crews, all part of the organization's live auction packages.

"Each fireman is an individual volunteer and not required to participate through his fire department or crew," says Lacey Sinn, development director.

How does she find participants?

"I have always recruited through personal contacts and have then moved to visiting individual fire departments, contacting local fire department chiefs for support," Sinn says. "And now that our event has taken place for three years, I also contact previous bachelors for recruiting suggestions. We have also had individual firemen contact us and offer to volunteer."

Bachelors are paired with an auction package that includes dinner for two and a local activity such as a movie, rock climbing, a magic show or outdoor concert.

For the 2009 event, bachelors and date packages were auctioned for $75 to $800, bringing in a total of $5,250. Bringing in an additional $3,510 were ticket sales — $25 in advance and $30 at the door. Admission included hors d'oeuvres, a hosted bar, professional photos with the bachelors and an after-party with a live band.

If your organization is interested in hosting a bachelor auction, Sinn offers the following suggestions:

- Solicit a well-known emcee. "We were lucky to have a local radio personality who has donated her time to the event as an emcee the last three years," Sinn says. "I would encourage anyone looking to do a similar event to search out someone like that. Not only did it give us a great emcee for our event, but it also gave us a lot of free promotion."

- Hire a professional auctioneer.

- Choose a location that permits outside catering. "If it is at all possible to find a location that will allow you to bring in your own outside catering and alcohol, do it," Sinn says. "It will save you thousands."

Source: Lacey Sinn, Development Director, Idaho Federation of Families for Children's Mental Health, Boise, ID. Phone (208) 433-8845. E-mail: lsinn@idahofederation.org

At a Glance —

Event Type:	Bachelor Auction
Gross:	$11,100
Costs:	$2,000
Net Income:	$9,100
Volunteers:	7
Planning:	120 hours beginning six months prior to event
Attendees:	157
Revenue Sources:	Ticket sales, live and silent auctions, cash donations
Unique Feature:	Hosted hors d'oeuvres, beer, wine and professional photographer who takes photos of attendees with bachelors

Content not available in this edition

Fundraising Auction Puts Member Talent Up for Bid

Consider showcasing the talents of your members in a creative way: Ask them to offer gift certificates related to those talents in gift baskets for your next fundraising auction.

This worked well for the February 2010 fundraiser for the Northfield Union of Youth (Northfield, MN) called I Heart NuY Fundraiser. The group's 900 members — all between the ages of 12 and 20 — worked to create a Valentine-themed event complete with a pre-Valentine's Day dance party, photo booth, pink cotton candy sales and more.

One key ingredient to the evening's festivities was the auction of donated gift baskets created by members that showcased member talents (e.g., dance lessons, bead-making lessons or home-cooked meals). The gift baskets were auctioned off during the event and proceeds went to the final bidder.

Source: Amy Merritt, Northfield Union of Youth, Northfield, MN. Phone (507) 663-0715. E-mail: northfieldunionofyouth@gmail.com. Website: www.unionofyouth.org

First Year of Online Quilt Auction Successful, Educational

With the proper planning, even first-year events can prove overwhelmingly successful in generating needed funds as well as awareness of a worthy cause.

Staff and supporters of the Ovarian Cancer Awareness Quilt Project at the University of Texas M. D. Anderson Cancer Center (Houston, TX) hosted its first online quilt auction in 2008. In that first year, the online auction of 68 hand-crafted quilts raised $11,440 for the Blanton-Davis Ovarian Cancer Research Program.

To promote fundraising efforts, a cancer center employee collaborated with local quilt stores with the goal of hosting an online quilt auction.

According to Pamela Weems, program director for community relations in the Department of Gynecologic Oncology at M. D. Anderson, the creation of quilts for this cause is sentimental, as many quilters have known someone who has lost a battle to ovarian cancer. Many of the quilts feature patterns that emphasize the cause with the use of the teal-colored awareness ribbon associated with ovarian cancer.

"Quilters who participate in this project share a love for the artistry of quilting," says Weems. "Many want to honor the memory of someone who battled ovarian cancer by designing a quilt in honor or memory of that person."

Weems shares tips for hosting an online quilt auction:

- **Attend local quilt shows and festivals** to learn how to properly display quilts and to promote your online auction.

- **Promote the event well in advance.** Some in the quilting community do not utilize computers, so mailings and media promotion are key to having a more advertised event. Approach local media to support your event.

- **Host a booth at local quilt shows and festivals.** Hand out flyers about your needs for the event including requests for quilt blocks and quilt donations. The Ovarian Cancer Awareness Quilt committee at M. D. Anderson prepared save-the-date cards in November 2008 for the October 2009 event.

- **Develop rules and deadlines** for the online auction. Provide these on your website.

- **Plan a community-wide quilting event** called a "Sew In" where quilters can gather to piece together donated quilt blocks and prepare to assemble quilts. This is also a good time to ask local news media to join you for promotion of the event.

- **Host an onsite viewing** at your organization of the quilts to allow the public a closer look of the quilts to be auctioned.

- **Create information cards for each quilt.** Cards can list the quilt's title and number, the name of the quilter who created it, how it was stitched (hand or machine) and other details important to the bidder. When posting images online for the auction, include these facts along with the size of the quilt.

- **Determine the value of each quilt.**

Source: Pamela Weems, Program Director for Community Relations in the Department of Gynecologic Oncology at The University of Texas M. D. Anderson Cancer Center, Houston, TX. Phone (713) 792-2765.
E-mail: gynonccommunityrelations@mdanderson.org

Auction Off Business Connections

Pulling off a successful fundraising auction is a challenge when the economy is down, as normally impulsive bidders may hesitate about spending the cash, especially for frivolous items.

Enter the auction of a valuable commodity: business leads.

The Michigan Council of Women in Technology (MCWT) of Auburn Hills, MI, raises up to $30,000 in a single event by auctioning off time with Michigan-based chief information officers at large corporations such as GM, GMAC, Ford, Lear Corporation and Comerica Bank.

"We've auctioned them off primarily to companies who want to do business with them — technology vendors like Compuware, Oracle, IBM, Information Builders and CSC," says Kathleen Norton-Schock, vice president of marketing at the council dedicated to increasing the number of women working in technological fields.

They auction the opportunities at two annual fundraisers — a golf outing and black-tie fundraiser. At the golf outing, bidders vie for the chance to play golf with company representatives. At the black-tie event, they bid to have dinner with them.

"We have more than 500 attendees, a number of whom work for information technology or telecommunications vendors or consultants — Microsoft, IBM, Oracle, Sun Microsystems — highly motivated to have lunch or dinner with a targeted CIO at a company with whom they already do business or want to do business," she says. "So we inform them via e-mailed newsletters a month ahead of time who will be up for auction. They internally strategize to decide on whom they want to bid."

Source: Kathleen Norton-Schock, Vice President of Marketing, Michigan Council of Women in Technology, Auburn Hills, MI. Phone (248) 335-4445.
E-mail: knorton-schock@ardentcause.org

Online Sports Auction Beats Event Planning for University

When it comes to raising funds, online auctions are hard to beat, says Whitey Rigsby, director, The V Club, Villanova University (Villanova, PA).

Through online auctions, "We've raised between $80,000 and $100,000 every year for the last five years, without the overhead or work involved with a large-scale event," Rigsby says. In fact, he says, for the first five years of the auction, responsibilities were so manageable that he and his secretary easily handled all of the necessary work.

The auction features sports memorabilia, vacation packages and once-in-a-lifetime opportunities, including the chance to travel with the men's basketball team to Louisville or be a Villanova Wildcat Ball Boy or Girl at a men's basketball game.

The three-week auction begins at the start of basketball season, right before Christmas. V Club officials guarantee all items will arrive by Christmas, which Rigsby says adds interest as people are able to bid on gifts for fans and alumni alike.

Villanova's sports teams are able to gain additional benefit from the auction by providing items of their own, with the net proceeds from these items going to their respective programs. For example, Rigsby says, the baseball team raised $30,000 for its program that way during the last auction.

Rigsby works with sports technology company Sound Enterprises (Norcross, GA), which handles the online aspect of the auction. The V Club pays Sound Enterprises 10 percent of auction proceeds and a 4-percent credit card fee, leaving 86 percent of funds raised to go directly to help support athletes and sports programs.

Like any auction, Rigsby says, the event is not without stress as organizers wonder what the results will be and whether all the work will be worth it. But after 10 years, he says, "We're at a point where we have resolved a lot of the issues and securing items is really more of a renewal process now than cold calling. Plus, we have a lot wider reach online than we would ever have at an event."

Source: Whitey Rigsby, Director, The V Club, Villanova University, Villanova, PA. Phone (610) 519-5505.
E-mail: whitey.rigsby@villanova.edu

Five Steps to a Successful Online Auction

The 10-year-old online auction for V Club of Villanova University (Villanova, PA) has a strong history of success, raising $80,000 to $100,000 each of the last five years. Whitey Rigsby, V Club director, shares some of what he and his colleagues have learned over the last 10 years to help make your online auction successful.

1. **Find the right company.** It may take a few tries before you find the best match for you. Rigsby says they worked with two or three other companies before finding their best partner in Sound Enterprises.

2. **Network, network, network.** This is the key to one-of-a-kind auction items and repeat donations.

3. **Timing is everything.** Plan your event at a time when you can piggyback on hype or tie into other events. The V Club auction runs between Thanksgiving and Christmas, at the start of the men's basketball season. Fans are pumped up about the new season and people are looking for Christmas gifts.

4. **Get specific.** For vacation home and timeshare items, clarify with the donor when the winner can use the prize. Make sure those dates and any supporting documentation are listed on the auction site. When notifying the winner, make sure to reiterate the dates the prize is available for use.

5. **Do it all at once.** Rigsby says some organizations have open-ended auctions, consistently offering one or two items all year long. "Limiting it to a certain time period allows momentum to build and creates a following. People can count on when the auction is going to be and they start to look forward to it."

Online Auction Companies Can Boost Success

A number of companies are devoted to helping nonprofits succeed at online auctions. Here are a few to check out as you search for the best match for your organization:

- Sound Enterprises — www.soundenterprises.net
- Bidding for Good — www.biddingforgood.com
- Idonatetocharity.org — www.idonatetocharity.org
- Charityfolks.com — www.charityfolks.com
- Charitybuzz — www.charitybuzz.com

Want to Make the Most of Your Silent Auction? Take it Online

Jon Carson, CEO of Bidding for Good (Cambridge, MA), knows how to make silent auctions work with optimum efficacy.

Carson's business hosts online auctions for nonprofits using techniques gleaned from extensive research. "In person," Carson says, "silent auctions just don't work like they should." However, when that auction is moved online: "The same pair of sports tickets that sold in a silent auction for $450 will sell for $600. It's a matter of supply and demand."

Carson explains how the Bidding for Good model works:

✓ **Timing.** According to Carson's associate Deepak Malhotra, assistant professor at Harvard Business School, live auctions are more successful than silent auctions because of competitive arousal. During a live auction, as stakes escalate, so does competitive excitement, making participants more likely to bid, and bid higher. Silent auctions do almost the opposite. Research shows people dislike betting against friends while socializing, and there is no climactic finish at the silent auction's close. "When you're at home viewing an online auction, that competitive arousal comes back," Carson says. "We know that in the last hour and a half of an online auction, bids spike considerably. It allows people to focus and get excited in a way they can't when they're writing on a clipboard in the middle of a crowded room."

✓ **Higher participation.** Auctions that are part of a gala event are only accessible to attendees of that event, who may represent only a fraction of the potential donor pool. Online auctions can reach anyone in the organization's community — and well beyond — at any hour of the day or night.

✓ **Searchable items.** When people are able to find items that they want and bypass items that they don't, they are more likely to bid.

✓ **Better donations.** Due to the above factors, online auctions reach a broad base of people who are ready and willing to spend. Therefore, online auctions become attractive platforms for companies to donate auction items simply for the advertising opportunity. Free product equals pure profit for your organization.

✓ **Targeted techniques.** An online auction is a controlled environment that can be tailored to bidders' behavior. For instance, studies show people are more likely to respond to bid alerts that appeal to their sense of charity rather than competition — until the auction is almost over. Another example: Research shows women bid on more items than men do, while men bid higher and more competitively than women do. Online auctions can take such factors into account to build them into auction set-up.

Source: Jon Carson, CEO, Bidding for Good, Cambridge, MA. Phone (866) 621-0330. E-mail: jon@biddingforgood.com. Website: www.biddingforgood.com

Raffles Prove Recession-proof for Fundraising

While creativity is a good thing, sometimes sticking with a proven event is better.

A prime example of this is the raffle. During a recession, a raffle accomplishes many things that bigger fundraisers usually can't. For instance, because people can get involved in a raffle for a relatively low cost, it can be a great way to attract first-time donors and increase your database.

Raffles also have staying power and can be held again and again, since for each one, the donor is not being asked to give much money or donate any time. People also like the nostalgic feel of raffles, especially during tough times. And from the perspective of development staff, raffles are practically free and very easy to operate.

The Appalachia Mission of Hope (McKee, KY), a Christian charitable organization, holds 12 or more successful raffles throughout the year. Even though the organization is located in an impoverished area, organizers say the raffles are a hit because ticket prices are set at only $1 per ticket, and because the prizes are always useful and enjoyable.

Ann Williams, director of operations, schedules raffles with holidays year-round, when people are more willing to spend a little extra in the hopes of having something nice for the holidays in return.

"In November, we raffle a huge basket of food items and gift certificate for a turkey or a Thanksgiving meal," Williams says. "For Easter, we raffle a basket stuffed with toys and goodies for a child. For Mother's Day and Father's Day, we raffle a basket of items for a lady and a basket of items for a man. In summer, we raffle a two-night stay at a motel coupled with tickets to some type of entertainment. We live some two-and-a-half hours from resort areas like Pigeon Forge and Gatlinburg, TN, so these locales work well for us."

Even without holiday themes, the mission has ongoing success raffling off dinner-and-a-movie packages. For a recent raffle, Williams collected gift certificates from seven restaurants and packaged them together into one raffle, she called Food for a Week.

One more mission-friendly trick about raffles is that they are an easy way to foster one-on-one relationships within the community. Williams prefers to sell raffle tickets at the mission's small thrift store, where volunteers can make face-to-face contact with members of the community.

Ann Williams, Director of Operations, Appalachia Mission of Hope, McKee, KY. Phone (606) 965-2449. E-mail: awilliams@amohonline.org

Star-driven Online Auction Draws Big Names, Funds

Project Paper Doll is the brainchild of folks at Monroe Carell Jr. Children's Hospital at Vanderbilt (Nashville, TN). The popular fundraiser engages famous musical artists Kenny Chesney, Carrie Underwood, Christina Aguilera and many more in creating paper doll artwork using common craft-making supplies.

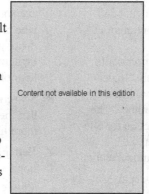

Content not available in this edition

The artists decorate and autograph wooden blocks shaped as two paper dolls holding hands to match the hospital's logo, and the star-studded designs are put up for auction on eBay to raise funds and awareness for the hospital.

Amy Crownover, the hospital's coordinator of eBay programs, answers questions on the successful online event:

How did you come up with this creative idea?

"The concept of Project Paper Doll came from a brainstorming session between community volunteers Traci and Bryan Frasher and our manager of music industry relations. It was inspired by Traci's vision that local celebrities would be willing to give a small bit of their creativity with an autograph to support Children's Hospital."

How do you connect with stars to create and autograph the paper dolls?

"Bryan Frasher is employed with a major record label and our music industry manager had many connections in the music industry through a former job. Together, they created a Project Paper Doll Committee that included numerous entertainment industry representatives."

How much was raised for this event and how many paper dolls were sold?

"In December 2007, 51 dolls were auctioned, which brought in bids totaling $21,143. In December 2008, 59 dolls were auctioned, which brought in bids totaling $22,273. The auctions were conducted solely online on the eBay platform. The Project Paper Doll series was heavily promoted by the eBay Giving Works Department through a printed catalog and webpage announcements on the eBay site."

This event took place in 2008. Did you have a 2009 Project Paper Doll as well?

"We chose not to have a Project Paper Doll event in the fall of 2009, so we could take some time to examine the program's great success and decide how best to build on it further. I expect the event to return very soon, in a more vibrant way."

What tips do you have for conducting an online auction to garner the most from bidders?

- "Create a unique item that cannot be recreated or purchased anywhere else.
- "Seek a commitment from celebrity participants to announce and promote their involvement to their fans.
- "Utilize volunteer labor and creative power to the fullest.
- "Seek in-kind corporate support for shipping, Web design, photography, etc., in exchange for online acknowledgement.
- "Be strategic in choice of celebrity involvement to maximize outcome — both revenues and exposure."

Source: Amy Crownover, Coordinator of eBay Programs; Laurie E. Holloway, Manager of Public Affairs; Monroe Carell Jr. Children's Hospital at Vanderbilt, Nashville, TN. Phone (615) 322-4747. E-mail: amy.crownover@att.net or laurie.e.holloway@Vanderbilt.edu. Website: www.vanderbiltchildrens.org

Boost Results by Combining Live, Silent, Electronic Auctions

How does the Gambit Auction and Dinner of Canisius High School (Buffalo, NY) raise around $300,000 every year? Its 36-year history helps, but so does offering a variety of auction events, says Colleen Sellick, Gambit program coordinator.

The fundraiser begins months before the night of the event as parents and alumni hold up to a dozen parties to gather the 500 to 600 items auctioned every year.

At the event, most gifts are distributed via silent auction. Items with bid sheets attached are displayed in five large groups that are progressively closed as the night proceeds. Larger items are reserved for the final group, and a grand finale offers a last chance at anything still available.

Following the silent auction, a live auction showcases two dozen of the most valuable and unusual gifts. Real-time action helps drive bids higher, says Sellick, and limiting the number of items offered helps retain interest and attention.

A gift website complements the traditional auction catalog as it displays all auction items and sorts them into categories to make navigation easier while allowing development staff to analyze the yield from different kinds of gifts and advise prospective donors accordingly. (Sellick says electronics, sports memorabilia, unique items and vacation homes generally offer great returns for their price.)

The school also began auctioning items directly online this year using the online Web service Maestrosoft. So far Sellick has simply sold the items outright, but notes that another option involves using the highest online bid as the starting bid for on-site live or silent auctions.

"We have received donations and bids from around the country," she says. "In the future, this will be a great way to reach beyond our immediate community. And for now, just getting the word out about this feature has driven people to the website and increased our direct online donations, which is a great start!"

Source: Colleen Sellick, GAMBIT Coordinator, Canisius High School, Buffalo, NY. Phone (716) 882-0466. E-mail: Sellick@canisiushigh.org

Auction Doubles Attraction With Bachelor Dates, Event Packages

An event that began as a former board member's idea has grown from a small gathering to a signature fundraiser for a Florida nonprofit.

In its seventh year, the Bachelor, Baskets and Services Auction to benefit the Community Service Council of West Pasco (New Port Richey, FL) combines the auctioning of dates with local bachelors with service packages to appeal to a wide variety of attendees.

"We have single women (or groups of women or offices) looking to buy a bachelor for themselves or single friends," says Becky Bennett, special events chair. "With the service packages, married and not-single women can come for the show of auctioning off the bachelors and still purchase great service packages. Even men come to this event and bid on service items."

This year, organizers put 13 bachelors and 12 service packages on the auction block. Funds raised go to scholarships for high school seniors, one adult scholarship and other projects the council does to benefit the community.

The bachelors ranged in age from 29 to 50-something and offered prospective bidders a wide selection of dates, including:

✓ Dinner and a comedy club.

✓ Kayaking, lunch and ice cream.

✓ Double date in a limo to a yacht ride followed by dinner, sunset cruise and dancing.

✓ Drinks at sunset from a balcony followed by a candlelit dinner, moonlit walk at the pier on the gulf, drinks and music at a local club.

The 12 service packages, each with a minimum value of $500, included:

✓ An enchanted evening package featuring a couples massage.

✓ A personal chef preparing a Couples Aphrodisiacs' Dinner at either the chef's restaurant or the couple's home.

✓ A pig-out and party package featuring a dinner for eight provided by a local barbecue restaurant and four hours of DJ service.

✓ A getaway package packed with a four-hour fishing trip, a round of golf for four at a local country club, two-month membership and 50 percent off group weight-training classes at the YMCA.

Bennett says the 2009 event raised a record $19,250. Bids on bachelors raised more than $4,000; service packages, $3,600; sponsorships, more than $5,900; ticket sales, $2,600; 50/50 raffle and Chinese auction, $2,000; diamond and ruby ring live auction, $410.

Source: Becky Bennett, Special Events Chair, Community Service Council of West Pasco, Hudson, FL. Phone (727) 967-7509. E-mail: bbennetthfpasco@aol.com

At a Glance —	
Event Type:	Bachelor & Services Auction
Gross:	$19,250
Costs:	$3,050
Net Income:	$16,200
Volunteers:	40-plus
Planning:	3 months
Attendees:	250
Revenue Sources:	Sponsorships, ticket sales, bachelor and service package auctions, live auction, 50/50 raffle, Chinese auction tickets
Unique Feature:	Offers dual attraction of bidding on dates with bachelors as well as couple and group-oriented outings

Seek Ways to Improve Event Each Year

To build on success, organizers of the Bachelor, Baskets and Services Auction for the Community Service Council of West Pasco (New Port Richey, FL) look for ways to improve the event year to year.

This year, for example, they put the auction stage in the middle of the room to give all bidders a good view and equal chance to bid on dates.

They also extended the beginning of the evening when guests could mingle and get acquainted with the gentlemen who agreed to put themselves up on the block.

Best Ever Directory of Special Events, Fifth Edition.
Edited by Scott C. Stevenson.
© 2010 Stevenson, Inc. Published 2010 by Stevenson, Inc.

HOLIDAY ORIENTED EVENTS AND FUNDRAISING PROJECTS

Holidays represent great times for events and fundraising projects of all kinds. Here's a sampling of holiday oriented events and projects.

Table Event Celebrates Holidays, Raises Awareness, Funds

Holiday-themed events can become family traditions and reliable, crowd-pleasing ways to raise funds and awareness for your cause.

Staff and supporters of the Susan B. Allen Memorial Hospital Foundation (El Dorado, KS) hosted its inaugural Holiday Tables event during the 2009 holiday season.

Held at the El Dorado Civic Center, the event allows local business and civic groups to showcase a tablescape to include elegantly adorned table linens, decorations and centerpieces all with a holiday or seasonal theme. Each organization is offered an 8-by-10-foot space and one table to decorate as they wish to demonstrate their spirit.

Table themes can be decorated in fall, winter, Easter, Fourth of July, Thanksgiving, Christmas or any other holiday or special occasion meaningful to the organization decorating that table. Additionally, participating organizations can post signage at their sponsored table to market their organization.

"One of our goals was to hold an event that had not been done in the community before and make it affordable for people to attend," says Mary Luebbert, director of development. "It is a great way to showcase some of our wonderful businesses and to bring out those people who love to decorate, professionally or as a hobby."

Ticket holders voted for their favorite table and ribbons were awarded to the winners. Attendees to the November 2009 event paid $30 to enjoy advance viewing of the tables along with wine and hors d'oeuvres, while tickets to the main event were $10.

This flyer helped draw participants and attendees to the inaugural Holiday Tables event for Susan B. Allen Memorial Hospital Foundation (El Dorado, KS).

Interested in trying a similar event to draw attention to your mission and raise funds for your organization? Here are three tips to make the event a success:

1. Advertise, advertise, advertise! Don't forget to publicize your event in local trade publications and newsletters geared to civic groups and professional organizations to attract more guests and table-decorating participants.

2. Make sure you complement the decorations with appropriate background or live music to inspire more event goers.

3. Don't forget to target local civic groups as potential participants to decorate a table.

Source: Mary Luebbert, Director of Development, Susan B. Allen Memorial Hospital Foundation, El Dorado, KS. Phone (316) 321-8741. E-mail: mluebbert@sbamh.org. Website: www.sbamh.org

Elegant Valentine's Event Promotes Romance

A couples-only evening may be just the ticket for your next special event.

For three years, the Isabella Stewart Gardner Museum (Boston, MA) has hosted a Valentine's Day filled with elegance and romance. At the 2009 Venetian Valentine event, 264 museum guests enjoyed live jazz, cocktails, fine art, self-guided Art of Romance tours and romantic delicacies such as oysters and chocolate-dipped strawberries. Tickets, available for advance purchase only, were $90 per person or $175 per couple for non-members (ticket price included a year of museum membership), and $65 per person or $125 per couple for museum members.

To offer a similar event packed with romance:

- Create ambiance with flameless candles, twinkle lights and soft music.

- Offer activities that can be completed in twosomes. The museum event offered an evening of romance with self-guided tours in its softly lit galleries.

- Select romantic foods and beverages to perpetuate the romantic atmosphere.

- Offer guests a parting gift that accentuates the theme. Guests departing the Venetian Valentine event were given a gift bag filled with romantic mementos and indulgent special offerings meant to ignite romance throughout the year. Included in the Venetian Valentine gift bag were a decadent cupcake from a local bakery, tulip bulbs from a local floral design company and a discount coupon at a local spa.

Source: Brittany Duncan, Publicist, Marketing & Communications, Isabella Stewart Gardner Museum, Boston, MA.

Ring in Holiday Spirit With Ornaments That Promote Your Cause

Now's the perfect time to begin planning your holiday fundraiser, especially if it involves ordering special merchandise such as holiday ornaments.

At Gaston Hospice and Grief Counseling Services (Gastonia, NC), a group of five volunteers ages 70 to 80 affectionately known as the "Wild Women" successfully managed the first-ever sale of ornaments to benefit the organization, says Jennifer Jones, volunteer coordinator. The premiere-event in 2008 featured snowflake, bell and ball ornaments handcrafted by regional potters.

"The Wild Women spent 150 hours of volunteer time preparing the ornaments for the sale," says Jones. "They packaged them and made them look beautiful. We couldn't have done it without them!"

Gaston Hospice offers the following tips for making an ornament sale a success:

1. Be careful not to order too many ornaments the first year to avoid cutting into profits. If you do have a surplus, offer extra ornaments at next year's sale. Many people enjoy collecting a series of ornaments and are willing to pay for past years' items to complete their collection.

2. Start out small and let the fundraiser grow year after year.

3. Ask local restaurants, gift shops and other retailers to display ornaments and distribute order forms to increase exposure of the ornament sale.

4. Publicize the event. Ask your local newspaper to run an article about your ornament sale and make sure you mention it in your newsletter as well. Also, send postcards and order forms to the people on your mailing list.

Source: Jennifer Jones, Volunteer Coordinator, Gaston Hospice and Grief Counseling Services, Gastonia, NC.
Phone (704) 861-8405.
E-mail: cunningj@gmh.org

This full-color postcard helped kick off the first-ever holiday ornament sale for Gaston Hospice (Gastonia, NC).

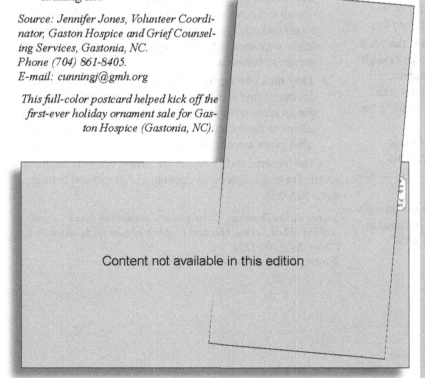

Content not available in this edition

Holiday Gift Wrap Raises Funds, Involves Community

The weeks between Thanksgiving and Christmas mean many things to many people, but to the residents of Cheyenne, WY, they mean volunteers from the Cheyenne Regional Medical Center will be wrapping piles of holiday gifts at the local mall.

"We're in our 29th year and still going strong," says Bev Catalano, volunteer director at the center.

Well-stocked with festive paper, bows and ribbon, volunteers wrap some 3,000 to 5,000 gifts in any given year, most for a fee of $3 to $5. And though center officials pay a minimum deposit and percentage of sales to the mall for use of an empty storefront or central booth, they still clear $10,000 to $17,000 every year.

What is the most difficult part of hosting a month-long fundraiser?

"Volunteers," says Catalano without hesitation. Though 100 or so are drawn from the center's active volunteer base, 150 more must be recruited from the community itself.

To meet this need, each of the fundraiser's almost 30 days has a day chair responsible for ensuring the booth is adequately staffed with workers Many of these volunteers come from the hospital staff itself, but day chairs also network through churches, clubs and other employers.

Because the three-decade-old event is well-known in the area, Catalano notes, it often draws groups of volunteers such as the employees of a bank, the members of a sorority or the staff of a local newspaper.

Though the fundraiser demands significant human resources, Catalano cites not only the sheer fun of holiday festivities, but also the chance to interact with the wider community as some of the benefits making the effort worthwhile.

"People's first question is always the cause we are raising money for," she says. "The gift wrap provides a great opportunity to increase awareness about the projects we're working on and the services we provide to the community."

Source: Bev Catalano, Volunteer Director, Cheyenne Regional Medical Center, Cheyenne, WY.
Phone (307) 633-7513.
E-mail: Bev.catalano@crmcwy.org

Author Lends Credibility and Substance to Event

St. Luke's Junior Auxiliary (SLJA) of San Francisco, CA, has hosted an annual holiday luncheon and boutique for 22 years. The event traditionally draws 400 guests and has raised from $20,000 to $80,000 each year.

For the 2009 event, organizers invited Kelly Corrigan, author of "The Middle Place," to speak and read from her best-selling memoir about her and her father's battle with cancer.

When working with a notable author for a special event, Amy Jones, president of the SLJA, offers the following tips:

✓ **Find an author or writer relevant to your audience or cause.** "Kelly was really funny and made the women in the audience both laugh and cry," says Jones. "She could really relate to our audience. She also shared some of her newest (then unreleased) book, for the first time ... so we felt honored to get a sneak peek."

✓ **Definitely connect with the author about what they will cover in their presentation and set expectations ahead of time.** Determine how many hours the author can devote to the presentation, mingle with guests and sign books.

✓ **Determine if there will be an author fee and build that into your budget.** Corrigan donated her speaking fee but typically does charge a fee. An author may request books be purchased for each guest of the event. In this case, the SLJA pre-purchased 300 books and sold them to members and guests, which Corrigan signed at the event.

✓ **Book an author well in advance of the event.** The demand for an author's time is extremely high, so plan ahead. The SLJA started conversations with Corrigan six months prior to the event, finalizing all details four months before the event.

Source: Amy Jones, President, St. Luke's Junior Auxiliary, Lafayette, CA. Phone (925) 588-5982. E-mail: amyrjones@gmail.com. Website: www.slja.clubexpress.com

How To Bring a Successful Event to the Next Level

For nine years, the holiday tea event at the Madison Children's Museum (Madison, WI) was a big hit — the largest of the museum's three annual events. But tough economic times called for tougher fundraising efforts, so staff decided to revamp their most popular event to earn an even bigger revenue.

Their efforts worked: In the three years since the revamp, the event has peaked at about $27,500 in net profits. Here's how the museum staff and supporters achieved this:

❑ **They changed the audience.** In earlier years, the event was a tea party geared toward female donors and daughters. Now called Tea and Trains, the event maintains the antique feel guests had grown to love, along with elements that appeal to boys as well as girls. Among the retooled event's crowd-pleasing features are:

• Story time, complete with a slide show of book illustrations. Volunteers read stories at intervals throughout the 3.5-hour event. All other activities are ongoing.

• Tea, cookies, chocolates and snacks, available throughout the course of the event. Catering staff included as part of the event rental maintain the snack table.

• A toy train table. The conductor (actually the owner of the elaborate model train set) donates his time.

• A silhouette center, silent auction, craft area and more.

❑ **They changed venues.** Before, they hosted the event in a smaller space that limited the event's scope. Moving to a larger space allowed them to invite more guests and encourage invitees to bring guests. The event now occurs in a private club, which maintains an elegant Victorian feeling. The cost of the club is one of the event's major expenses, but is discounted due to the event chairperson's connection to the club.

❑ **They took photographs.** In changing an existing event, documentation is essential for helping new and returning guests know what to expect. A photographer donated his talents to the museum and allowed use of the photos in other promotional materials.

The museum staff's efforts are paying off, with the most recent Tea and Trains event drawing 417 guests and netting some $25,000.

Source: Adam Erdmann, Development Coordinator, Special Events and Individual Giving, Madison Children's Museum, Madison, WI. Phone (608) 268-1231. E-mail: aerdmann@madisonchildrensmuseum.org.

Best Ever Directory of Special Events, Fifth Edition.
Edited by Scott C. Stevenson.
© 2010 Stevenson, Inc. Published 2010 by Stevenson, Inc.

Think outside the box as you select special events that will be distinctively yours and help draw attendees who might otherwise say no to another run-of-the-mill event. Be mindful of who you want to reach — and what it will cost to attend — in choosing an event.

Twitter-driven Event Draws Crowd in 15 Days

Pulling off the first-ever HoHoTO (Toronto, Canada) event — a party at Toronto's Mod Club in support of the community's food bank — was no small feat.

In just 15 days, the Toronto technology community generated enough interest for the event to raise $25,000 for the Daily Bread Food Bank, solely by using their connections and marketing the event via Twitter. The event is pronounced hoe-hoe-TEE-oh, in recognition of the holiday season and Toronto's nickname, T.O.

Co-organizer Michael O'Connor Clarke offers tips for making a Twitter-generated event more of a success:

A single tweet probably won't do it.

"That's not how Twitter works. For ideas to take off on Twitter, you need a network effect to happen — the idea has to spread organically, picking up traction and repetitions along the way. For this, either the idea must be highly compelling and impactful, or you need a lot of people to get behind the idea. You need to be able to reach a broad network of interested people who will spread the news for you."

You can't create network effects overnight.

"No organization should expect to be able to jump into Twitter (or other social media channels such as blogging, Facebook, YouTube, etc.) and immediately see benefits. It takes time to build a community of followers, friends and interested parties who will help you to get the word out when you have something to say. Start now — if you're not already active on Twitter, you should be. You need to become immersed in the community you're going to want to influence; it's the only way to really understand it. If you don't get it (and a lot of people just don't — that's OK) then hire someone who does."

Spend a lot of time listening.

"Before you engage with a Twitter audience, you need to understand who they are, what they're talking about, what they're interested in, whom they follow, what motivates them, what they dislike. There are lots of monitoring services and search engines you can use to do your research before you dive in. The thing is: Social media is about conversation. These conversations are multi-faceted, bidirectional and already happening. If you just jump into a conversation that's already going on without spending the time to listen to what's being said, you're only going to annoy people and your efforts will backfire."

Think through policies and processes.

"Once you engage online, you're going to find fans and critics. Nonprofit groups know they can polarize audience opinions quickly. So be prepared. What will you do when someone starts criticizing you online? How will you handle attacks? Will you respond? If so – who responds, how, and in what form? How do you deal with well-intentioned but off-message fans? This is a complex area — seek out a consultant who has done this kind of work for other nonprofits or organizations and ask for their help. It will be worth it."

Offer something of value.

"The incentive with HoHoTO was to have a great holiday party and be able to do some good at the same time. We created something of meaningful value for the community, and they rewarded us by showing up and giving very generously for the Daily Bread Food Bank. Simply tweeting about your great cause is not enough to really sustain people's interest — even the most charitable of us are still a little self-centered. With so many demands on our time and our pocketbooks, there has to be something valuable and worthwhile to make people want to really engage."

Source: Michael O'Connor Clarke, Vice President, Thornley Fallis Communications, HoHoTO, Toronto, Ontario, Canada. Phone (416) 471-8664. E-mail: mocc@thornleyfallis.com

OMG! Agency Raising Funds Via Texting

On Oct. 24, 2009, Louisiana State University (LSU) of Baton Rouge, LA, played Auburn University (Auburn, AL) in football at LSU's Tiger Stadium, but the real winner was Capital Area United Way (Baton Rouge, LA).

That's the day United Way staff and supporters took a leadership role in the move to incorporate mobile technology into fundraising efforts by capturing donations by text message.

To do so, the organization teamed up with mGive.com (a service of Mobile Accord, Denver, CO); Diane Allen & Associates Advertising & Public Relations, Inc. (Baton Rouge, LA); and LSU Athletics, giving donors the opportunity to instantly react to a fundraising appeal and confirm their donation by sending a text.

During the football game, LSU used game announcements and a Jumbotron ad to ask the 90,000 attendees to each donate $5 to Capital Area United Way by texting the letters "LSU" to 864833. Donations were charged to texters' monthly cell phone bills and identified as a non-taxable donation.

The event brought in $8,550 with more than 2,558 text messages sent. More than 800 people did not confirm the required second step in the text message donation process, so Profita asked fans to go back and ensure they confirmed. This resulted in an additional $465 in donations, bringing the total to $9,015.

Source: Karen Profita, President/ CEO, Capital Area United Way, Baton Rouge, LA. Phone (225) 346-5817. E-mail: karenp@cauw.org. Website: www.cauw.org/content/ ways_to_give

Brassiere Fashion Show and Auction Turns Heads, Raises Funds

Brainstorming for a unique way to raise funds for the CarePartners Hospice Foundation and for the Hope Chest fund of Hope Women's Cancer Centers, event organizers tapped into an attention-getting idea — a brassiere fashion show and auction.

Classy Bras for Sassy Broads featured a Brassieres on Parade Auction in which women volunteers from the community, ages 16 to 54, modeled bras, halters, corsets and other tops created by area artists and designers. Organizers say the event was tastefully done while still turning heads and gaining attention community-wide.

The event drew nearly 150 guests at $35 each, raising $5,600 from ticket sales and live and silent auction items that complemented the theme of pampering women including spa packages, jewelry and gift bags. The local Hooters restaurant sponsored the event, with two of its employees greeting guests at the door.

Kristie Quinn, event coordinator and planner, shares tips she learned through the new event:

❑ Draw people with an eye-popping invitation. Organizers of the Classy Bras for Sassy Broads event worked closely with a trusted graphic design company to create the stunning invitation at right.

❑ When setting a deadline for creative submissions, realize that artists and designers tend to work up to the deadline and typically work well under deadline pressure. Schedule buffer time in to your event schedule to allow for this aspect of working with a creative team.

❑ With a fashion show auction as the main event, communicate clearly with guests on how bidding works. Allow ample bidding time.

❑ Have designers invite guests to the show. Whether those guests are interested bidders or just there to support the artist, friends and family of that artist should cheer and express their enthusiasm to energize the crowd while the artist's piece is on the runway.

❑ When obtaining sponsorship from a local restaurant or business, tap the main office or headquarters of that chain to land larger sponsorship support. For a brassiere fashion show, ask the main office to design a top for the event, ask the head office to suggest potential models from their staff and/or ask for major sponsorship.

Source: Kristie Quinn, Event Coordinator and Planner, CarePartners Hospice Foundation, Asheville, NC. Phone (828) 277-4815. E-mail: KristieQuinn@aol.com

Content not available in this edition

Partners Are the Toast of Upscale House Party

Wine and children are not a combination you normally hear about, but the Loop 360 Circle of Friends Pairing of the Vines event made wine pairings pay off for Dell Children's Medical Center (Austin, TX).

The event, hosted at the home of U.S. Congressman Michael McCaul and his wife, Linda, featured food, wine and martinis from Sullivan's Steakhouse. The restaurant's donation of all items helped the event raise more than $15,000 for the hospital's mental health component.

Since the Circle of Friends organization did not have funds budgeted for the event, the event depended on the generosity of area businesses, says Jayme Clark, Circle of Friends coordinator. That's where positive prior connections paid off.

"In coordinating numerous events, we have created partnerships with businesses that understand our mission and want to get involved. There are so many ways to give back to the community other than monetary. During these tough economic times, our partnerships have continued to support us through in-kind donations for which we are very grateful."

Partners' donations were maximized by combining them to create memorable auction packages (e.g.; a pair of airline tickets might be matched up with a weekend stay somewhere or a private wine tasting for 12 at a vineyard).

Clark says they also managed to maximize the exposure partners got, promoting them in as many ways as possible. For instance, sponsor and auto mogul Roger Beasley, created quite a buzz, parking an Audi, Maserati and Porsche outside of the McCaul's home during the event.

"It's important to benefit the business that is generously giving and promote them as much as possible," Clark notes. "Partnerships become a win/win when the partners are respected, taken care of and considered part of your fundraising family."

Source: Jayme Clark, Circle of Friends Coordinator, Dell Children's Medical Center, Austin, TX. Phone (512) 324-0170. E-mail: jsclark@seton.org

Celebrate the Unusual for Unforgettable Fundraising Festivals

They say when life hands you lemons, make lemonade. Apply that philosophy to fundraising to put a fun, festive spin on an event or situation that people typically dread.

Take, for example, blackfly season, which hits Vermont each spring.

"At times, the air is so full of blackflies that they fly up your nose and into your mouth when you breathe," says Karen Kane, co-president of the Adamant Cooperative (Adamant, VT), the state's oldest non-profit food co-op.

So a few years ago, the co-op's members collectively brainstormed and decided to make the most of the situation ... by making blackfly pie! Since that year, the Blackfly Festival has reaped financial and marketing rewards for the organization's fundraising and outreach.

The first festival took place seven springs ago, in what Kane says organizers saw as "a day-long festival that would bring joie de vivre to the battle between insect and human."

Now held each May, the festival is the organization's key fundraiser and signature community event. It brings in thousands of dollars in a single day and is also a huge PR boost. "We get in all the local media, plus out-of-town media. This gives us credibility that ads can't buy," Kane says.

The event unites the entire community — and visitors from across the country — to celebrate "the bug we love to hate," she says. Numerous participatory events include a BFF parade — which they call the Macy's Day Parade of the Insect World — featuring eclectic costumes and performances of synchronized bug zappers. A Blackfly Pie contest is judged by chefs from the nearby New England Culinary Festival. A nature walk along Sodom Pond, the source of the bugs, sheds light on these pesky-yet-celebrated creatures.

Since it's a food co-op, it's no surprise that Adamant makes the most of the event by selling food, including black bean burgers from the grill. The group's secondary revenue stream comes from its Blackfly store: bug salve, tennis racket-shaped bug zappers, T-shirts, caps and bug bafflers (screened, hooded shirts that keep the flies away from the face).

What makes the event such an effective fundraising and marketing tool, Kane says, is that "the festival has kind of a cult following. Most come for the pure zaniness of it; others come out of curiosity; a few are legitimate bug enthusiasts."

And where the people go, the press follows. "A writer from the Wall Street Journal came to the festival one year," says Kane, "and there was a photographer from Travel + Leisure, plus a great video that ran on a Vermont newspaper's website in 2007 — all of which have helped spread the word."

Source: Karen Kane, Co-President, Adamant Cooperative, Adamant, VT. Phone (802) 223-5760. E-mail: karen@parisbydesign.com. Website: www.blackflyfestival.org

---

Tap These Fun, Fresh Fundraising Ideas

Want to raise money and get some great publicity? Host one of these unusual fundraising events:

1. **Grown-Up Spelling Bee:** Everybody loves a spelling bee, especially if it gives adults a chance to relive their grade school glory days! Raise money with participant entry fees and/or audience tickets. Add in a silent auction, concessions and baked goods on the side. If your first spelling bee goes well, consider monthly playoffs with a year-end championship bee.

2. **Bring Your Dog to Work Day:** How much do you think a dog lover would pay for the privilege of having his/her furry friend at work? If your agency locale is not appropriate, seek out a supportive business to host a premiere event, with hopes it grows in popularity throughout your service area as workers pay a donation to your cause to have Fido come along on a casual Friday. For extra fundraising, ask nearby pet stores for donations, such as gourmet dog biscuits, snazzy collars or other gift items to be sold on-site that day, or see if a dog grooming salon would be willing to donate its services for an afternoon. Another option if all-day dog visits are out of the question: Host a pet parade or a lunch hour get-together at the local dog park.

3. **"No Dirty Dishes For A Week" Raffle:** This fundraising idea is all about the marketing. Rather than having people go to others' houses to wash dishes, it involves securing gift certificates for seven area restaurants — from casual to formal — to create a raffle package good for a full week of dinners. Whether offered community-wide, as part of a larger raffle or in-house at a business supporter of yours, this raffle is sure to draw positive publicity and much bidding action!

Extreme Fundraising Goes Over the Edge

A year ago the staff of Special Olympics Missouri (SOMO) was looking for a fundraising event that would be fresh, new and big.

Little did they know that the event they sought would turn out to be bigger than a 20-story building.

More than 12 months, several site safety plans, and many conference calls later, the organizers recently completed the last of four Over The Edge rapelling events.

These hair-curling fundraisers offered any fan able to raise a minimum of $1,000 and brave enough to attempt the feat the opportunity to rappel down buildings, including the 10-story State Office Building and a 20-story casino.

"We do a lot of fundraisers," says Ashley Dawson, SOMO development coordinator. "But this is just so unique. The media loves it, and we've really benefited from the exposure."

The four events were produced in partnership with Over The Edge USA (Athens, GA), a company that specializes in rappelling fundraisers. "They take care of all the technical details and day-of logistics, while we handled finding the buildings, recruiting participants and generating publicity," says Dawson.

Months of planning were kept on track by a benchmarked timeline, frequent conference calls and a best-practices manual provided by Over The Edge.

The events were valuable not only for the buzz they created, but for the diversity of participants as well, says Dawson. The participants included those who consistently support the Special Olympics; those who love rappelling and rock climbing; and those who simply want a once-in-a-lifetime experience.

The three groups were about equal in terms of numbers represented, she says, estimating that as much as 50 percent of the participants had never before supported the Special Olympics chapter.

All told, 169 "edgers" took the plunge at one of the four sites, raising around $170,000 for a worthwhile cause.

While expenses exceeded SOMO's standard cap of 30 percent of revenue raised, Dawson looks to improve the profit margin in future events through corporate sponsorships and other means.

"We're already looking for locations for next year," she says. "It's definitely something we are going to pursue."

Source: Ashley Dawson, Development and Volunteer Coordinator, Special Olympics Missouri, Jefferson City, MO.
Phone (800) 846-2682. E-mail: Dawson@somo.org

Content not available in this edition

Take Your Event Over the Edge

Since offering their first "drop zone" in 2003, Over The Edge USA (Athens, GA) has assisted dozens of nonprofits to raise funds in a unique, thrill-inducing way.

Partnering with a range of charities, Over The Edge provides technical expertise, including:

✓ rappelling experts
✓ all necessary equipment
✓ $5 million insurance certificate
✓ comprehensive event manual that includes the best practices from more than 20 marketplaces

For more information, go to: http://overtheedgeusa.com

A participant in the Special Olympics Missouri's Over The Edge! rappeling event descends a wall. Offering the experience at four sites helped the organization raise $170,000.

Let Your Supporters Take a Leap for a Good Cause

A successful special event is one that not only raises funds for your cause, it leaves participants and spectators alike talking about it in a positive way for weeks to come.

Since 2004, Gap Adventures and Planeterra (both Toronto, Ontario, Canada) have worked together to sponsor an annual Jump for Charity where brave souls skydive to raise funds to support Planeterra's mission. These unique events offer jumpers and spectators alike a day of thrills while raising money and awareness for Planeterra.

Gap Adventures is a worldwide adventure travel company that offers socially and environmentally sustainable travel to all seven continents. Officials with Gap Adventures founded Planeterra — a nonprofit organization dedicated to development and support of small communities around the globe — and conducts these skydiving events to raise funds to support the organization.

Liz Manning, Planeterra's sustainability manager, answers questions about their Jump for Charity events:

When did you start hosting skydiving fundraisers?

"The skydiving event was launched in July of 2004, and we've held five each July with the last in 2008. Tony Cook, our sales manager, is an avid skydiver and has a close connection with a local drop zone and the event grew out of that

relationship and our desire to have a creative, original and adrenaline-fueled event."

How many skydivers participated in the most recent event? How many spectators?

"The last few years we've averaged 40 skydivers and more than 100 spectators at each event."

How are funds raised at the event and how much was raised at the 2009 event?

"Gap Adventures, Planeterra's founder, covered the cost of the skydive fees and we asked participants to actively fundraise. We awarded prizes for top fundraisers including a Gap Adventures tour. Our last Jump for Charity raised over $20,000!"

What is the top innovative tip you could share with another organization about trying a similar event?

"Get creative with marketing to appeal to a wider audience and those who are more inclined toward adrenaline-fueled fun, but you would be surprised the mix of ages your participants will have. One of my favorite participants was an incredibly dynamic and energetic grandmother!

Source: Liz Manning, Sustainability Manager, Planeterra, Toronto, Ontario, Canada. Phone (416) 260-0999. E-mail: liz@planeterra.org.

Make Humor the Center Attraction for Your Special Event

Nothing gets people on your side — or the side of your cause — more than giving them a reason to smile and laugh.

For nine years, humor has taken center stage at Roast-a-Doc, the primary annual event for Sutter Davis Hospital Foundation (Davis, CA).

Roast-a-Doc has become a much-anticipated event throughout the region, says Kristine Stanfill, director of development at the foundation. The event is dubbed "stimulating entertainment with fiery wit" where, each year, a doctor from the organization is selected to be the focus of a roast in the name of good fun and to raise needed funds for the hospital by way of ticket sales and an auction held at the event.

Changing things up a bit this year, two doctors — Dr. Arfan Din and Dr. Kraig Katzenmeyer — were featured in March 2010 receiving the brunt of the good-natured jokes from colleagues, friends and family. The two doctors were selected to be roasted as a team as they are frequently seen together at the hospital.

"The roast is a fantastic event in that it incorporates community members, physicians, staff, grateful patients and volunteers," Stanfill says. "We deliver an event that generates funds as well as builds lasting relationships and we have an opportunity to honor our mission publicly — a win-win on all levels."

Follow these tips for hosting a successful roast event at your organization:

Content not available in this edition

- Use messaging that is simple, yet recognizable. By designing a distinct logo for this special annual event, recipients of invitations and other communications about the event instantly identify with the logo and know the communication piece is about the Roast-a-Doc event.

- Work with an independent event coordinator team. Roast-a-Doc event organizers hire two local independent event planners who plan the bulk of the event. Using independent event planners allows for more flexibility and using local planners helps the event to draw on more local sponsors to support the event.

- Invite the guest of honor to select where the proceeds from the evening will be allocated. In return for being a good sport as the focus of the roast, the medical professional who is the object of the roast determines which area of the hospital will benefit from the proceeds and enthusiastically engages in the outcome and success of the event.

Source: Kristine Stanfill, Director of Development, Sutter Davis Hospital Foundation, Davis, CA. Phone (530) 750-5220. E-mail: StanfilK@sutterhealth.org. Website: www.sutterdavis.org

Art and Soup Event Proves to Be a Profitable Recipe

For the Visiting Nurse Association (VNA) of Omaha, NE, combining delicious homemade soups with unique artwork is a recipe for success.

In February 2010, the VNA hosted its 13th annual Art & Soup event. The celebration proved to be the most successful event to date, raising more than $140,000 to benefit public health services for children and adults living in homeless shelters in the Omaha area.

For the Art & Soup event, the VNA collaborates with local restaurants and artists to acquire unique food and art pieces. Some 55 artists and 31 restaurants participated in the 2010 event. Artists donate 50 percent of proceeds from artwork sales during the event to support the cause. Most participating restaurants create and premiere signature soups just for the event.

Organizers say restaurateurs clamor to feature a soup at the event because of the exposure it gives their business. Restaurateurs also participate in anonymous judging, vying for awards, including people's choice.

The VNA's Operation Frontline staff also prepares a low-cost soup for the event to share what a typical soup kitchen may serve. Operation Frontline is a collaborative venture between the VNA and Share Our Strength (Washington, D.C.) — a nonprofit that weaves together a net of community groups, activists and food programs to reduce hunger among children — that links local chefs and dietitians with people who are at risk of hunger and malnutrition.

Held at Omaha's Holiday Inn Convention Center, the event begins early in the afternoon with a patron party. For $100 a ticket, patron party attendees enjoy hors d'oeuvres, soups prepared by Sage Student Bistro at the Institute for the Culinary Arts, live music and artist-staffed creation stations where guests create their own artwork. Patron party attendees also enjoy early entrance to Art & Soup, buy-it-now on the silent auction, meet artists one-on-one and purchase original artwork.

Two hours later, the doors open for persons who paid $45 in advance or $50 at the door. The guests all may visit the ballroom lined with tasting stations featuring soups of all exhibiting restaurants, vote for their favorite, view and purchase original art from area artists, enjoy desserts and coffee and listen to live jazz music.

Source: Betty Cernech, Vice President of Community and Public Health, Visiting Nurse Association, Omaha, NE. Phone (402) 342-5566.
E-mail: bcernech@thevnacares.org.
Website: www.thevnacares.org

At a Glance —

Event Type:	Soup tasting event combined with hands-on art exhibits
Funds Raised:	$140,000
Attendees:	1,000
Revenue Sources:	Ticket and patron party sales; art sales; silent auction; corporate sponsorships/donations
Unique Feature:	Local restaurants share signature soups as artists sell artwork

Breweries Add Local Interest To Tour of Homes

Look to add community flavor to your annual tour of homes to pique interest and draw in a fresh audience.

After 42 years of hosting the Tour of Historic Galena (IL) Homes, the Galena-Jo Daviess County Historical Society was running low on options for new locations. So when owners of a home that housed a historic brewery and sat next to the old city brewery offered their residence for the tour, planners' wheels started turning.

"The cellars provided a whole different type of architecture that really drew people in," says Colleen Yonda, assistant director of the society. "You don't usually see vaulted brickwork and limestone arches in events like these."

Organizers worked to leverage these added layers of interest, with 100-plus volunteers providing costumed interpretation, explaining the history of beer making. The owner of a local microbrewery worked with the historical society to offer a tasting of locally produced ale and lager, while a local merchant offered coupons for locally brewed beers, with a portion of the sales going to the historical society.

The weekend event attracted more than 800 participants and raised around $6,500 for the society.

Source: Colleen Yonda, Assistant Director, Galena - Jo Daviess County Historical Society. Phone 815-777-9129.
E-mail: info@galenahistorymuseum.org

Unique Tour Ideas

Consider these tour options to spice up your fundraising efforts:

✓ Kitchens — Remodeled or historic, there's something for any cook or homeowner.

✓ Penthouses/High-rise condos —— View life from the top.

✓ Churches — Experience the sacred and serene.

✓ Gardens — What better way to pass a summer evening?

✓ Green buildings — Visit the area's most eco-friendly structures.

✓ Ponds — Fountains, reflections and bridges, always a warm-weather favorite.

✓ Lighthouses — Explore local history and connect with the culture of the sea.